ONE TRUE GOD

UNDERSTANDING
LARGE CATECHISM II.66

EDWARD ENGELBRECHT

CONCORDIA PUBLISHING HOUSE · SAINT LOUIS

Copyright © 2007 Concordia Publishing House
3558 S. Jefferson Ave., St. Louis, MO 63118-3968
1-800-325-3040 • www.cph.org

Written by Edward Engelbrecht

This publication may be available in Braille, in large print, or on cassette tape for the visually impaired. Please allow 8 to 12 weeks for delivery. Write to the Library for the Blind, 7550 Watson Rd., St. Louis, MO 63119-4409; call toll-free 1-888-215-2455; or visit the Web site: www.blindmission.org.

Manufactured in the United States of America

1 2 3 4 5 6 7 8 9 10   15 14 13 12 11 10 09 08 07 06

CONTENTS

PREFACE

I began writing the first part of this study document when the Commission on Doctrinal Review asked for clarification of the wording in Large Catechism II 66 provided in *Concordia: The Lutheran Confessions* in light of a challenge questioning it. At that time I provided a document that contained (1) examples of some of Luther's German sentences from the Confessions, (2) a brief explanation of what we had noticed about Luther's use of the subjunctive mood and concessive conjunctions in these sentences, and (3) the need to make the rhetoric of the passage clear for people who were not accustomed to reading Luther.

As you can see, the document has changed as we sought greater clarity with the Commission. Nonetheless, still in place are the basic points that guided our translation of this challenging passage in the Large Catechism.

THE LARGE CATECHISM

Every Lutheran studies the Small Catechism. Luther's Large Catechism is less well known and perhaps requires some introduction for lay readers. Both catechisms were published in 1529 and present essentially the same body of doctrine. Their bones are certain passages that summarize biblical teaching (Ex 20; 1 Cor 15; Mt 6; Mt 28; Jn 20; Mt 26, etc.). Ancient and medieval teaching exercises gave the catechisms their question-and-answer format. The order of the passages and the style of the explanations are wholly from Luther: plain spoken and compelling, pessimistic about human reason and strength, but fully confident in the Gospel.

The catechisms grew up together from three series of sermons Luther preached from May 1528 to March 1529. The Small Catechism gives the basics. The Large Catechism fills in details from Scripture and from evangelical counsel. Luther believed that a person could never outgrow the content of the catechisms and encouraged people to study them as a part of daily prayer.

STUDYING THE LARGE CATECHISM

Like many graduates from Concordia Seminary, I studied the Large Catechism with Prof. Jerold A. Eickmann during my first classes on the Lutheran Confessions and Christian doctrine. Later I studied the Large Catechism in German with a reading group led by Dr. Wayne Schmidt, who was a professor at Concordia Seminary, taught Theological German, and also served on the catechism committee for The Lutheran Church—Missouri Synod (the committee that produced the 1991 edition of *Luther's Small Catechism with Explanation*). I scheduled the meetings for the reading group. Dr. Schmidt assigned passages from the German Large Catechism out of the *Concordia Triglotta*. During the week participants worked through the passages independently and then took turns translating in the reading group. As we worked through a passage, Dr. Schmidt would comment on Luther's grammar, word choice, and rhetoric. (I do not recall whether we studied LC II 66 at that time.)

To be candid, I did not organize the reading group because I was interested in sixteenth-century German. While pursuing my STM, I wanted to read German articles and commentaries on the Bible and the early Church fathers. It was Dr. Schmidt's idea that we study Luther's German Catechism together as the most fruitful means for growing in our knowledge of German and Lutheran doctrine. Also, at that time I was working with tools for Reformation research as a library reference assistant and as a research assistant for Dr. Normal Nagel, who was chairman of the department of Systematic Theology. If the present document proves helpful for understanding Luther's comments in Large Catechism II 66, Eickmann, Schmidt, Nagel, and others deserve much of the credit since they encouraged me to study Luther. Of course, they should bear no blame for weaknesses in this document.

AN EXPLANATION FROM DOGMATIC THEOLOGY

While finishing this study document, I asked for the permission of Concordia Publishing House's publisher and executive director of our editorial division, Rev. Paul T. McCain, to include the second part (pp. 91–108), "Luther, the Lutheran Confessions, the Holy Scriptures, and LC II 66." Paul prepared this document at the invitation of the Commission on Doctrinal Review. He did the important work of gathering numerous passages from Luther's writings, which were very valuable to me as I developed my paper for the commission (see especially Chapter 5).

Since Paul's letter was a dogmatic treatment of the topic, I thought it valuable to include. It will also give readers a glimpse of how the publishing house worked with the commission on this matter.

A WORD OF THANKS

I must thank my colleagues at Concordia Publishing House and the many peer reviewers who suffered through earlier drafts of this document and provided helpful feedback. They challenged my assumptions and compelled me to dig deeper. Librarians David Burger and Jean Baue also offered excellent help in gathering resources. Also, special thanks are due to members of the Missouri Synod's Commission on Doctrinal Review, who patiently read different versions of the manuscript and commended its publication for study.

May the Lord bless your prayerful consideration of this challenging topic.

Rev. Edward A. Engelbrecht, STM
Senior Editor, Professional and Academic Books
Concordia Publishing House

ABBREVIATIONS

AE   *Luther's Works*, American Edition

AC   Augsburg Confession

Ap   Apology of the Augsburg Confession

BKS   Bekenntnisschriften der evangelisch-lutherischen
            Kirche

CTLC   *Concordia: The Lutheran Confessions*

CR   *Corpus Reformatorum*

Ep   Epitome of the Formula of Concord

FC   Formula of Concord

K/W   Kolb and Wengert, *The Book of Concord*

LC   Large Catechism

SA   Smalcald Articles

SC   Small Catechism

SD   Solid Declaration of the Formula of Concord

Tappert   *The Book of Concord*

Tr   Treatise on the Power and Primacy of the Pope

Triglotta   *Concordia Triglotta*

WA   *Luthers Werke*, Weimar Edition

Part 1

HISTORICAL THEOLOGY

Chapter 1

INTRODUCTION

*Almost immediately after the release of the book, for-
mal challenges were submitted to the Commission on
Doctrinal Review.*

—Report from the Commission on
Doctrinal Review, January 2006

Since 2001, the meaning and application of Large Catechism (LC) II
66[1] has been a matter of considerable discussion and controversy
among Lutherans in North America. Several articles have been published related to this passage:

- The Faculty of Concordia Theological Seminary, "Religious
Pluralism and Knowledge of the True God," *Concordia
Theological Quarterly* 66, no. 4 (October, 2002): 295–305 (see
especially 299–300).
- Charles Arand and James Voelz, "Large Catechism, III, 66,"
Concordia Journal 29, no. 3 (July 2003): 232–34.
- John Nordling, "Large Catechism III, 66, Latin Version,"
Concordia Journal (July 2003): 235–39.
- Thomas Manteufel, "What Luther Meant," *Concordia Journal*
(October 2003): 366–69.

- E. Christian Kopff, "Who Believes in and Worships the One True God in Luther's Large Catechism?" *Logia: A Journal of Lutheran Theology* XIII, no. 3 (2004): 55–57.

Each of these publications provides some comment on the Latin and/or German texts. The Latin text is most carefully explained in the articles by Nordling and Kopff. Most explanations of the German text have focused on the lack of the definite article in the phrase "only one true God" ("nur *einen* wahrhaftigen Gott").[2]

REASONS FOR CONTROVERSY

Despite these helpful publications, the German text of LC II 66 remains controversial. Here is the text as translated in the *Concordia Triglotta* (Triglotta):

> For all outside of Christianity, whether heathen, Turks, Jews, or false Christians and hypocrites, although they believe in, and worship, only one true God, yet [they] know not what His mind toward them is, and cannot expect any love or blessing from Him.[3]

The text remains controversial because the concessive conjunction (*ob . . . gleich*) could be translated "although," "even though," or "even if." Also, the verbs "believe" and "worship" (*glauben* and *anbeten*) are not clear grammatically. These verbs could be in the indicative mood or in the subjunctive mood.[4] Both interpretations of the verbs have been offered. Settling the mood of these verbs could be critical for understanding the passage. However, one could even argue that their mood is not critical! In any case, the grammar of LC II 66b has been the focus of discussion to the neglect of other important aspects of the passage.

SMALL CHANGES

One may rightly ask, "Do the differences in wording described above really matter?" They matter because the differences in wording lead to very different theological statements. The nature of these differences can be illustrated by the following sentences:

- Non-Christians believe in and worship only one true God.
- Non-Christians do not believe in and worship only one true God.
- Non-Christians may believe in and worship only one true God.

These sentences, with slight differences in wording, say very different things. For the sake of comparison, consider how differently the following statements might sound to one's spouse:

- I do love you alone.
- I don't love you alone.
- I may love you alone.

As these examples illustrate, small changes in wording can have a remarkable effect on meaning!

Also, one could note in a pragmatic way that the differences in wording certainly mattered to those who brought charges of false doctrine against the publication of *Concordia: The Lutheran Confessions* (CTLC). The charges were important to the editors of the book, if for no other reason than that tens of thousands of people were using it. The differences likewise mattered to the Commission on Doctrinal Review, which desired to clarify the issue. These reasons alone were enough to warrant a careful study of the passage.

However, the concerns mentioned above were motivated by still deeper concerns. The controversial sentence in LC II 66 was being used more and more in doctrinal discussions, and it touched on numerous points of doctrine, such as the following:

- The nature of the Church (Ecclesiology)
- Natural knowledge of God (General Revelation)
- Revealed knowledge of God (Special Revelation)
- The power of human will and reason (Anthropology)
- The effects of original sin (Hamartiology)
- Grace (Soteriology)

- Faith and justification (Soteriology)
- Worship (Sanctification)
- Eternal punishment (Eschatology)

The controversial sentence also touched on a number of practical issues that lay people and church workers face:

- Proclaiming the Gospel to non-Christians (Missions/ Evangelism)
- Marriage to non-Christians (Teaching and Counseling)
- Explaining the First Commandment and the Creed (Catechesis)
- Public or civic gatherings for prayer (Worship)

Though some theologians were advocating that the passage should not be cited in theological discussions because it was unclear, this counsel was not being heeded. People were naturally forming opinions about the passage and then citing the passage in support of their view. The church's need for greater clarity drove the development of this study document. The Commission on Doctrinal Review requested its publication.

THESIS

In LC II 66 Luther argued forcefully that Christians are the only people on earth who genuinely believe in and worship the one true God. The following points of evidence will demonstrate this thesis:

- Historically and theologically, Luther had carefully considered the scholastic issue of whether non-Christians believe in and worship the one true God.
- Dialectically and rhetorically, Luther argued against the conclusion that some non-Christians can actually believe in and worship the one true God.
- Grammatically, Luther frequently used contrary-to-fact concessive clauses for dialectical and rhetorical arguments, such as the argument in LC II 66.

- Careful analysis of the clause in LC II 66b, in view of its broader context, leads one to interpret and translate the clause as contrary to fact.
- Arguments for a statement-of-fact interpretation of LC II 66b do not account for the historical, theological, dialectical, rhetorical, and grammatical evidence. In fact, to date no one has published an argument explaining or defending a statement-of-fact interpretation of the concessive clause in LC II 66b.

A preliminary conclusion will appear at the end of each chapter. The final portions of the book will draw together all aspects of the investigation for a comprehensive analysis of the German text of LC II 66.

You do not need to know German or Latin in order to understand the essential arguments of this book. But knowledge of those languages will prove especially helpful. The goal of this publication is to investigate the German text thoroughly in view of its broader context so that the Church may reach a clearer understanding of what Luther was saying in this passage. (Please note: the focus on the German text is not meant to reject the authority and use of the Latin text.)[5]

AN IMPOSING FORTRESS

Reading this book may be compared to assaulting a medieval fortress. This is because the topics addressed here are, indeed, medieval. The topics Luther studied as a young student—grammar, rhetoric, and dialectic—seem distant and granite-hard for many readers today. Though you have studied grammar and composition in school, it is not likely that you studied these topics as Luther did. As you will discover, Luther was a master of late medieval composition and style.

The first chapters are not too difficult, like crossing green fields and pastures. Anyone who enjoys history or theology will walk through these chapters relatively easily. However, the sixth chapter is the outer wall of the fortress. It presents a substantial challenge to the reader who has not studied formal logic. Don't give up. Many readers will need to work through this section more than once in order to grow confident about its archaic terms and categories.

The seventh chapter is less difficult. Though the formal study of rhetoric is not common today, people of all eras are acquainted with the art of persuasion.

The eighth and ninth chapters are the high tower of the fortress. Unless you are familiar with sixteenth century German grammar or linguistics, it may feel like you are scaling this tower with an uncertain grip, like rock climbing with chain mail gloves impeding your feel for Luther's language. To encourage you for the climb, this section introduces Luther's use of concessive conditional clauses with a line from his most loved hymn: "A Mighty Fortress Is Our God." If you patiently work through this section, you will discover that, beyond the stony surface of the grammatical evidence, there is great reward for the reader: a deeper understanding of this prince of theologians.

Take note: changes in German grammar have contributed to the confusion about LC II 66. The particular concessive conjunction Luther used in the sixteenth century is not used in the same way in modern German. If you try to use a modern German dictionary to interpret the passage, you will likely be misled. (These issues will be described in detail by Chapter 8.) Also, it is worth noting that dictionaries and grammars are by nature general information. To understand the wording and grammar of a particular author, such as Luther, you need to study what he does in his writings. Throughout the book there will be references to a collection of appendices (pp. 109–148). These materials are the building blocks for the study, cut from *Luthers Werke* (Weimar Edition [WA]), the American Edition of *Luther's Works*, *Corpus Reformatorum*, and the *Concordia Triglotta*.

The tenth through twelfth chapters take account of the fields, wall, and tower you have scaled. They apply each topic for the interpretation of LC II 66, survey various proposals for translation, and weigh counterarguments. The conclusion describes theological implications. (As mentioned in the author's preface, an explanation from dogmatic theology was provided by Paul T. McCain on pp. 95–108.)

NOTES

1. It seems that even the reference system of the Large Catechism is controversial, since some designate the passage as LC, III, 66. This book uses a traditional

reference system: document, chief part, paragraph number. References to "66b" mean the second sentence in paragraph 66.

2. W. H. T. Dau and F. Bente, eds., *Concordia Triglotta* (St. Louis: CPH, 1921), 696–97. Unless otherwise indicated, all quotations of the Confessions are from the *Concordia Triglotta*.

3. *Triglotta*, 697. The German text is "Denn was auszer der Christenheit ist, es seien Heiden, Türken, Juden oder falsche Christen und Heuchler, ob sie gleich nur einen wahrhaftigen Gott glauben und anbeten, so wissen sie doch nicht, was er gegen ihnen [wie er gegen sie] gesinnt ist, können sich auch keiner Liebe noch Gutes zu ihm versehen" (694, 696).

4. Three English translations render the verbs as subjunctives. One modern German edition updates the passage as subjunctive. Six English translations are more or less ambiguous, allowing both indicative and subjunctive interpretations. See Appendix E. Also, a helpful point for the English reader is that the noun for God in German (*Gott*) is typically capitalized. German doesn't distinguish the true God from false gods by capital and lower case letters as in English. Luther's spelling and capitalization can vary considerably. At times he has "*gott*" when referring to the true God.

5. The 1584 Latin edition, edited by Martin Chemnitz, has long been regarded as the final, generally received Latin edition and the best commentary on the 1580 German text of the *Book of Concord*. See *Die Bekenntnisschriften der evangelisch-lutherischen Kirche*, 6th ed. (Göttingen: Vandenhoek & Ruprecht, 1967), XLIV. Pages 73–74 provide further comment on the relationship between the German and Latin texts of LC II 66.

Chapter 2

THE SETTING OF THE LARGE CATECHISM

The deplorable, miserable conditions which I recently observed when visiting the parishes have constrained and pressed me to put this catechism of Christian doctrine into this brief, plain, and simple form. How pitiable, so help me God, were the things I saw. . . . Yet all the people are supposed to be Christian . . .

—Martin Luther, Preface to the Small Catechism

In LC II 63–70 Luther demonstrated the unique teaching of the Apostles' Creed in distinction from the beliefs and teachings of other religions. He explored what it meant to be "Christian." Luther needed to make this point because of his broader concerns in the late 1520s about the future of Christianity over against heresies and other religions.

THE LATE 1520S

In 1525 the leaders of Europe began forming military leagues in case the Muslim Turks invaded. Like many Christian leaders in Europe, Luther was concerned about the spread of Islam and the future of Christianity. Luther was also concerned about the spread of false doctrine. The struggle with violent Anabaptists reached a crescendo in the Peasants' War (1525). During that same year, Luther wrestled with the teachings of the Renaissance humanist scholar, Desiderius Erasmus (ca. 1469-1536), on the freedom or bondage of the human will. In February 1527 the Swiss reformer Ulrich Zwingli (1484–1531) directly attacked Luther's teaching on the Lord's Supper, which resulted in a series of exchanges on the topic. In December 1527, when Luther participated in the visitation of Saxon churches, he discovered the deplorable state of parish education.[1] Luther saw that many of the people were barely Christian in their understanding and that many priests were unprepared to train the people in the faith. These latter observations were the specific motivations for Luther to begin work on the catechisms in 1528.

Between May 1528 and March 1529, Luther preached his catechetical sermons, which became the basis of the catechisms. In personal terms, by 1529 Luther's son Hans was old enough to begin learning his letters and numbers. Luther's family was growing, and so were the families of his colleagues. His letters at this time are full of references to pregnancies and births. Luther had to think personally and seriously about what it meant to teach the faith to the next generation and how that generation stood in relation to other religious groups. While writing the Large Catechism, Luther was also writing "On War against the Turk."[2] In April 1529 the Large Catechism came off the press.

A UNIQUE PEOPLE BY GOD'S GRACE

All these events form an important context for understanding Luther's writing about the Creed and faith in the Large Catechism. Through teaching the faith,[3] he was—by God's grace—establishing a unique people in the world:

> For although the whole world with all diligence has endeavored to ascertain what God is, what He has in mind[4] and does, yet has she never been able to attain to [Latin: the knowledge and understanding of] any of these things. But

here [in the Creed] we have everything in richest measure
... (LC II 63)[5]

In the Large Catechism, Luther acknowledged the religious and philosophical pursuits of all people, yet he concluded that they had not ascertained "what God is, what He has in mind and does" (LC II 63b). For example, in explaining the First Commandment, Luther observed,

> As I have often said that the confidence and faith [*Glaube*] of the heart alone make both God and an idol. If your faith [*Glaube*] and trust be right, then is your god also true [*recht*]; and, on the other hand, if your trust be false and wrong, then you have not the true [*rechte*] God; for these two belong together, faith [*Glaube*] and God. That now, I say, upon which you set your heart and put your trust is properly your god. Therefore it is the intent of this commandment to require true faith [*rechten Glaube*] and trust of the heart which settles upon the only true God [*den rechten einigen Gott*], and clings to Him alone [*allein*]. (LC I 3–4)[6]

THE WEAKNESS OF HUMAN REASON AND THE WILL

Luther believed that Christians could not boast of their own reason or strength in the matter of knowing God and His intent towards them (SC II, art. 3). Like all humanity, they were powerless to ascertain "what God is, what He has in mind and does" (LC II 63b). As Luther concluded in LC II 65:

> For (as explained above) we could never attain to the knowledge of the grace and favor of the Father except through the Lord Christ, who is a mirror of the paternal heart, outside of whom we see nothing but an angry and terrible Judge.[7]

The difference between Christians and non-Christians was not in their natural knowledge of God or their ability to pursue knowledge of God by reason or strength. The difference was in knowing God through His Son alone. Everyone without knowledge of the Son was outside genuine knowledge of the Father. In this way, faith in the Gospel (i.e., the Creed) established the boundaries of Christendom.

> But outside this Christian Church, where the Gospel is not, there is no forgiveness, as also there can be no holiness [sanctification]. Therefore all who seek and wish to merit holiness [sanctification], not through the Gospel and forgiveness of sins, but by their works, have expelled and severed themselves [from this Church]. (LC II 56)

A DIFFERENT FAITH HAS A DIFFERENT GOD

In the May 23, 1528, catechism sermon on the Apostles' Creed, Luther stated,

> Now [suppose] someone were to ask: "What kind of God do you have? What do you expect from Him? Since the gods of the pagans and of the Jews may be so diverse, do you also boast of your God, that He gave the Ten Commandments to you?" The Creed serves this [purpose and explains]: That's who He is, that's how He's named, that's what He does, etc. The Ten Commandments say nothing except, "you shall not have . . ." etc. Even the Jews and pagans also confess this. But which of the two is true God—theirs or ours? Then comes our Creed and leaves nothing out, because it concerns our faith, that is: The Christian Faith. . . . So the Creed is nothing other than an answer to this question: what kind [of God] is your God, who brought the Ten Commandments to you? By this faith we are separated from all other people, who do not have it [faith], because they have another god, etc.[8]

Luther prepared the Large Catechism from this sermon and other sermon series on the catechism. The passage quoted above appears to be the basis for Luther's comments in LC II 63–70. See Appendix A for further comments on this important sermon, which has not been translated into English before.

Conclusion

While writing the Large Catechism, Luther was thinking broadly about the future of Christianity in relation to other religions and religious movements. In LC II 66 he was not arguing abstractly but considering the concrete differences between Christianity and these other religions. This point is confirmed by the content of his May 23, 1528, sermon on the Creed. At the root of Luther's argument are the issues of what people can know of God and His mind toward them (i.e., the dogmatic topics of revelation, anthropology, and the results of original sin).

Notes

1. See the preface to the Small Catechism (SC), *Triglotta*, 533–39.
2. He finished the document in 1529. Luther supported military opposition to Turkish invasion. See the forthcoming book by Adam S. Francisco, *Martin Luther and Islam: A Study in Sixteenth Century Polemics and Apologetics* (Leiden: E. J. Brill, 2007).
3. The German word for "faith" (*Glaube*) is also the word for "creed." Dogmaticians distinguish "faith that believes" (*fides qua*) and "the faith in which ones believes" (*fides quae*). Luther associated faith and creed so closely with one another that in some passages it is difficult to discover which one he was writing about or whether he meant to distinguish them at all.
4. That is, God's attitude, whether He will be gracious or condemnatory.
5. "Denn alle Welt, wiewohl sie mit allem Fleisz dannach getrachtet hat, was soch Gott wäre, und was er im Sinn hätte und täte, so hat sie doch der keines je erlangen mögen [können]" (*Triglotta*, 694; the Latin includes, "*intelligentia aut ratione*"). In the studies thus far, LC II 63b has not been cited as necessary context for what Luther is arguing in LC II 66b. The significance of LC II 63b will be drawn out further in the sections on theology and dialectic.
6. G. Ebeling noted that Luther is not describing knowledge of God but the matter of honoring God. "Was heißt ein Gott haben oder was ist Gott?" *Wort und Glaube*, vol. 2, *Beiträge zur Fundamentaltheologie und zur Lehre von Gott* (Tübingen, 1969), 292. Ebeling distinguished two questions in Luther's explanation of the First Commandment: (1) What God is, and (2) What it means to have a God. The first question must be answered before the second.
7. "Denn wir könnten (wie droben erklärt) nimmermehr dazu kommen, dasz wir des Vaters Huld und Gnade erkennten ohne durch den Herrn Christum, der ein Spiegel ist des väterlichen Herzens, auszer welchem wir nichts sehen denn einen zornigen und schrecklichen Richter" (*Triglotta*, 694).
8. Translation by Edward Engelbrecht. See Appendix A.

Chapter 3

THE BORDERS OF
CHRISTENDOM, PART A

Perhaps the Spirit of Christ diffuses itself farther than we imagine; and that there are more Saints than we have in our Catalogue.

—Erasmus, *The Colloquies*

This chapter will provide background for the theological content of LC II 66 and help identify Luther's opponent(s). This history will illustrate what Luther stated in LC II 63b and will also show that passage's importance for Luther's argument in LC II 66b.

EARLY CHRISTIAN BACKGROUND

In LC II 63–70 Luther was rejecting the belief of some theologians that non-Christians could truly know and believe in the one true God through natural knowledge of God and philosophical reasoning.[1] The apostle Paul had already confronted this issue in the New Testament (cf. Acts 17:22–31; Rom 1:19–21). His texts were foundational to Christian thinking on this topic. Paul taught that the people of the Old Testament were saved through faith in Christ, who would appear in the future. After Christ came, people were saved through the proclamation of the Gospel (Gal 3). Though Paul wrote about the natural knowledge of God (natural revelation), his focus was always on the Law and the Gospel of Holy Scripture (special revelation).

The early Christian apologists also considered the issue of the natural knowledge of God. Some early Christian thinkers concluded that great philosophers (e.g., Socrates, Plato, Aristotle, and others) attained knowledge of the true God in part through *logic* (the divine Logos—Christ—manifested in the created order; Jn 1:1–4) but also through the teachings of Moses passed down through the Egyptians to the Greeks (e.g., Eusebius's *The Preparation for the Gospel*). In other words, they traced the excellence of human wisdom back to the special revelation of God's Word through His prophets.

In *The Consolation of Philosophy*, the early Christian writer Boethius (ca. 480–ca. 524) went in a different direction. He claimed that a person could attain knowledge of God and His mind toward humanity through reason. Boethius wrote his treatise entirely from pagan philosophical arguments without any reference to Scripture or Christ.[2]

MEDIEVAL BACKGROUND

Boethius's work became very influential in the early medieval era. His views were later supplemented with the teachings of Aristotle, which became available through Muslim scholars such as Avicenna (980–1037) and Averroes (1126–98). Scholastic theologians drew on all of these influences in considering the role of the natural knowledge of God in salvation.

The comparative study of religions (e.g., Roger Bacon, ca. 1214–ca. 1292) and greater metaphysical speculation (e.g., John Duns Scotus, ca. 1265–1308) prepared the way for "natural theology," attempts to derive knowledge of God and Christian doctrines from nature and reason alone.[3] The late scholastic theologians William of Occam (ca. 1285–1347) and Gabriel Biel (ca. 1420–95) rejected the belief that reason could produce a "natural theology." However, Biel and other scholastics taught that any person might be able "to do that which is in him" (*facere quod in se est*) and thereby attain "acquired faith" (*fides acquisita*).[4] These opinions would have a formative influence on Luther and other sixteenth-century theologians.

RENAISSANCE HUMANISM

The late medieval poet Dante (1265–1361) would become an important influence on the emergence of the Italian Renaissance and humanism. In the *Inferno*, Dante wrote that the noblest pagans would spend eternity in the highest level of hell, removed from the bitter sufferings others would experience (Canto IV). Like Dante, some humanists began teaching that the greatest thinkers and writers from antiquity would receive special treatment in eternity.

An expression of the Renaissance interest in reconciling Christianity and classical philosophy appears on facing walls of the Stanza della Signatura, the room in the Vatican where Pope Julius II (1503–13) would sign papal briefs. Raphael (1483–1520) painted on one wall the *School of Athens*, with Plato and Aristotle standing at the center. On the opposite wall he painted the *Disputa*, featuring a scholastic disputation with theologians and philosophers about the nature of the Sacrament of the Altar. These paintings powerfully illustrate the growing stature of pagan philosophy and its integration with theology at the dawn of the Reformation.[5]

Thomas More (1478–1535), in book two of *Utopia* (1516), expressed admiration for the nobility of pagan religious ideas and their compatibility with Christianity.[6] Desiderius Erasmus would become a hero to many Reformers, most notably the Swiss. In a dialogue for the *Colloquies*, he placed the following ideas on the characters' lips:

> Whatsoever is pious, and conduces to good Manners, ought not to be called profane. The first Place must indeed be given to the Authority of the Scriptures; but nevertheless, I sometimes find some Things said or written by the Ancients; nay, even by the Heathens; nay, by the Poets themselves, so chastly, so holily, and so divinely, that I cannot persuade myself, but that when they wrote them, they were divinely inspired; and perhaps the Spirit of Christ diffuses itself farther than we imagine; and that there are more Saints than we have in our Catalogue. . . . I never read anything in a Heathen, that comes nearer to a Christian, than what Socrates said to Crito, a little before he drank his

Poison . . . I can scarce forbear, when I read such Things of such Men, but cry out, *Sancte Socrates, ora pro nobis*; Saint Socrates, pray for us.[7]

Erasmus alluded to the view among the early Christian apologists that the Divine Logos was inspiring these noble pagan thinkers. He seems to reason that, if the Logos inspired them, then He must also have approved them.

CONCLUSION

Some ancient and medieval theologians taught that non-Christians could come to know, believe in, and worship the one true God apart from the message of Christ. Renaissance humanism placed renewed emphasis on this doctrine as it celebrated human reason and ability. Desiderius Erasmus was a key advocate of these teachings at the time of the Reformation. Although Luther's comment in LC II 66 may seem to address the opinions of these thinkers, the next chapter will describe an even more likely opponent.

NOTES

1. That Luther was forming an argument and not just thinking abstractly will be clarified in the sections on dialectic and rhetoric.
2. Boethius's work is a profound apologetic statement, but since it does not base its arguments and conclusions on the Scriptures, it should not be the basis of a Christian doctrine of God.
3. Bacon and Scotus did not conclude that the heathen had genuine faith, but their methodology prepared the way for such a conclusion. Cf. Philip Schaff, *History of the Christian Church*, vol. V (Grand Rapids: Eerdmans, 1984), 685, 697.
4. Heiko A. Oberman, *The Harvest of Medieval Theology: Gabriel Biel and Late Medieval Nominalism* (Durham, NC: The Labyrinth Press, 1983), 468.
5. Peter and Linda Murray, *The Oxford Companion to Christian Art and Architecture* (Oxford: Oxford University Press, 1996), 503–5. Lewis W. Spitz notes that the German Humanist Nicholas Cusanus (1401–64) was "pacific and conciliatory toward Islam and other non-Christian religions" (p. 174). *The Renaissance and Reformation Movements, Revised Edition* (St. Louis: CPH, 1987).
6. *Utopia: A New Translation, Backgrounds, Criticism*, trans. Robert M. Adams (New York: W. W. Norton & Company), 78–88.
7. *The Colloquies of Erasmus*, trans. N. Baily (London: Reeves & Turner, 1878) 1:182–86. Published August 1, 1524, at Basel, Switzerland. This colloquy is called

"The Religious Treat." According to the *Encyclopedia Britannica*, "The Dutch Humanist Erasmus (ca. 1466–1536) and others, however, went further in stating that the ancient thinkers had a direct knowledge of the highest truth and sometimes in comparing them favorably with Scholastic theologians. One of the interlocutors in his *Convivium Religiosum* suggests that it would be better to lose the Scholastic theologian Duns Scotus than the ancient Roman thinkers Cicero or Plutarch, while another speaker restrains himself with difficulty from praying to the Greek philosopher Socrates (ca. 470–399 BC) as though he were a Catholic saint." N. Sm. *Encyclopedia Britannica*, 15th ed. (Chicago: Encyclopedia Britannica, Inc., 1984) Macropaedia Vol. 15: 616.

Chapter 4

THE BORDERS OF
CHRISTENDOM, PART B

*If Scipio and Numa Pompilius, who were idolaters, have
been saved, why was it necessary for Christ to suffer and die,
and to what end is it necessary for Christians to be baptized
and for Christ to be taught? So horribly do men fall when the
Word has been neglected and laid aside, and they know
nothing about faith . . .*

—Martin Luther, AE 8:134

Like other sixteenth-century theologians, Luther was certainly
touched by Renaissance humanism. But as a biblical scholar and
an Augustinian, he did not adopt humanism's optimistic view of
human nature and reason. Nor did the natural knowledge of God play
such an important part in Luther's theology. Although Luther believed
in the natural knowledge of God's existence as described in Romans
1:20–21, he emphasized the importance and necessity of Scripture
alone for knowing God and God's "mind." He likewise emphasized
faith in Christ alone for knowing who God is.[1] By rejecting reason's
ability to produce a natural theology (cf. Rom 1:21–23), Luther made
a firm statement about the relationship between Christianity and

other religious beliefs such as those of "pagans, Turks, Jews, or false Christians and hypocrites" (LC II 66b).

In the *Disputation Against Scholastic Theology* (September 1517) and the Heidelberg Disputation (May 1518), Luther attacked the scholastic doctrine that a person could "do that which is in him"[2] and merit God's grace. He emphasized that human reason and the human will are corrupted by sin and therefore incapable of truly knowing God or pleasing Him.

Erasmus attacked Luther's teaching in his treatise *The Freedom of the Will* (1524). Luther refuted Erasmus on this point in the famous treatise *The Bondage of the Will* (1525). Erasmus responded with yet another treatise (*Hyperaspistes*, 1526). But Luther didn't even bother to answer Erasmus, since he regarded him as a spent force who would not find support among the Romanists or the Reformers. In the late 1520s, Luther turned his attention to the doctrines of the Swiss Reformers.

THE DOCTRINE ABOUT PIOUS HEATHEN

Zwingli came to a conclusion about the "pious heathen" (fromme Heiden) that was very different from Luther's.[3] Zwingli and other Swiss theologians reasoned that the noble heathen could truly know God even though they had not learned of Christ.[4] These theologians were more deeply touched by humanism and admiration for Erasmus,[5] though they did not fully agree with Erasmus's views. In 1526 Zwingli wrote,

> What do we know of the faith each one has written in his heart by the hand of God? Who does not admire the faith of that holy man Seneca, as his letter XXXIV to Lucilius discloses it? . . . Who, pray, wrote this faith upon the heart of man? Let no one think that these things point to the taking away of Christ's office, as some men charge me with doing; they magnify His glory.[6]

Zwingli held that people whom God predestined to salvation could exercise their God-given reason and will in seeking God, even though they knew nothing of the promised salvation in Christ.

Zwingli's dependence upon the doctrine of predestination for his view is not always evident in his statements about the pious heathen. Because he focused on the nobility of these persons, his statements appear to attribute their salvation to human faithfulness or merit. Modern historians, such as Rudolf Pfister, have had to write explanations of Zwingli's view on this point.[7] One can easily understand how theologians contemporary with Zwingli would be confused about what he was teaching.

Note how Zwingli complains in the quotation that others had learned about his opinion and charged him with false doctrine. His views were spreading in the mid-1520s and being critiqued by other theologians.

LUTHER'S CONCERNS ABOUT THE SWISS

Luther's letters from the late 1520s show his concerns about Zwingli and other Swiss theologians (WA Br 3 and 4). In September 1524, Carlstadt fled to the Swiss after he was expelled by the Saxon authorities for his radical teachings and activities. In November 1524, the Lord's Supper became an issue between the Lutherans and the Swiss; it remained the dominant issue throughout the 1520s. Luther concluded that Carlstadt was spreading his false opinions about the Lord's Supper and other doctrines.

In 1525, Luther assessed Zwingli's teachings and learned more about doctrinal issues between them. In a letter to Gottschalk Crusius, dated October 28, 1525, Luther condemned Zwingli's argument about the certainty of faith and attributed Zwingli's teaching to Carlstadt. About a week later (November 5, 1525) he warned the preachers at Strassburg about Zwingli's doctrine of original sin. In a report from ca. November 1525, based on a discussion with Luther, Gregor Casel summarized Luther's assessment of Zwingli (WA Br 3, 610). Much of the report is about the problem with Carlstadt. But Luther had clearly been studying Zwingli's writings and stated that "Zwingli never knew Christ" and he erred in the most important article of original sin. Luther noted that Zwingli depended far more on reason and did not "give room to the Holy Spirit." These doctrinal issues are among the very issues Luther addressed in LC II 66.[8]

In the spring of 1527, Luther published "That These Words of Christ, 'This Is My Body,' etc., Still Stand Firm against the Fanatics," which addressed issues that Zwingli and other Swiss theologians raised. Luther wrote,

> [Zwingli] will keep on and attack still other articles of faith, as he already declares with flashing eyes that baptism, original sin, and Christ are nothing.

The translator and/or editors for AE 37 saw in this quotation a reference to Zwingli's doctrine about the pious heathen as well as problems in Christology revealed by his doctrine of the Lord's Supper.[9] Later in the treatise Luther wrote,

> This is the rancor and hatred of natural reason, which wants nothing to do with this article [about Christ] and therefore spits and vomits against it, and then tries to wrap itself in Scripture so that it may avoid being recognized. Not a single article of faith would remain if I followed the rancor of reason. . . . With this rancor, however, my dear fanatics prepare the way for the virtual denial of Christ, God, and everything. In part, already, they have made a start at believing nothing at all. They follow the fancy of reason, which they expect to lead them aright. But this scoffing only serves the purpose of stirring up the foolish masses, who do not trouble themselves with Scriptures. They themselves know perfectly well that all their heathenish vomiting proves nothing against this article, or if it disproves this one, it also disproves all articles.[10]

Luther clearly saw the dependence of the Swiss upon "natural reason" and "heathenish vomiting," which could only lead to a denial of Christ.

In March 1528, Luther published the "Confession Concerning Christ's Supper," which more thoroughly addressed the issues raised by the Swiss. Luther again suspected Zwingli of "pagan" views because of problems in his Christology. Luther wrote,

I testify on my part that I regard Zwingli as un-Christian, with all his teaching, for he holds and teaches no part of the Christian faith rightly. He is seven times worse than when he was a papist. (AE 37:231)[11]

The timing of the "Confession" document is important because it appeared only about three months before Luther's May 23 sermon on the third article of the Creed, which is most likely the basis of his comments in LC II 66 (see Appendix A). In the "Confession," Luther wrote,

Outside of Christ death and sin are our masters and the devil is our god and lord, and there is no power or ability, no cleverness or reason, with which we can prepare ourselves for righteousness and life or seek after it. On the contrary, we must remain the dupes and captives of sin and the property of the devil to do and to think what pleases them and what is contrary to God and his commandments.

In this passage Luther described the "god" of those who are "outside of Christ" ("ausser Christo," WA 26, 503 [see also p. 507]; cf. LC II 56, 66 "Ausser der Christenheit," that is, "outside of Christendom"). Their god is the devil. In contrast with Zwingli and others, Luther had firmly concluded that if a person did not have Christ, he did not have the true God.

DIFFERENT FROM UNIVERSALISM

It needs to be stated that the doctrine taught by Zwingli and other Swiss Reformers was not universalism.[12] Some writers on this topic seem confused about this point. For example, in AE 55, the index volume, there is an entry regarding "universal salvation." The passages from Luther referenced in this list are tied to one another by the theme of "universal." But in many ways, the passages do not belong together.

In one passage, Luther referred to the view that all people including the devil would be saved. This is genuine universalism, which was not a significant issue for Luther and the Reformation.[13] Some of the passages refer to comments by Luther on 1 Timothy 2:4, that God "desires all people to be saved." These passages are not about universalism. In these passages Luther does not teach that all will finally be saved and that hell will be empty. Another passage listed is Luther's comment about Zwingli's doctrine that the pious heathen would be saved. This is also not universalism since Zwingli did not teach that hell would be empty and all would be saved. As noted above, Zwingli's doctrine about the "pious heathen" is rooted in his teaching about predestination.[14]

In LC II 63–66, Luther was not arguing against universalism, which did not become a significant issue of theology until the eighteen century. Luther was focused in this section of the catechism on (1) the distinction between Christians and non-Christians and (2) the abilities of human reason and the will (i.e., theological topics such as the nature of the Church, revelation, anthropology, and the effects of original sin). The argumentation turned on the Creed (*Glaube*; the Faith). As in his writing about what it means to "have a God" (LC I 1–4), Luther here wanted to distinguish what Christians have and know and what non-Christians lack.[15]

Christians have:	Non-Christians do not have:
The Creed	Knowledge of what God is
All our wisdom	Knowledge of what God has in mind
Everything in richest measure	Knowledge of what God does
Everything in heaven and upon earth	Expectation of God's love or blessing
His Son	The Lord Christ
The Holy Spirit	Illumination
Knowledge of the Father's grace and favor	Gifts of the Holy Spirit

According to LC II 63–66, the one thing about God that non-Christians clearly understand is that He is "an angry and terrible Judge." In LC II 66b, Luther conceded a ridiculous situation where people who have nothing but wrath and condemnation somehow have the one true God. In other words, Luther introduced an absurd argument in order to illustrate his main point: "These articles of the Creed divide and separate us Christians from all other people on earth" (more on this in the sections on dialectic, rhetoric, and grammar).

WARNINGS ABOUT ZWINGLI

It is not absolutely clear when Zwingli's opinion, expressed at least as early as 1526, became fully known to Luther. Luther was obviously reading Zwingli's writings in the 1520s.[16] The two theologians were at odds throughout 1527–28.[17] The passages cited show that Zwingli's dependence upon humanistic views were noted well before Luther wrote the catechisms and could have prompted his argument in LC II 63–70. Gottfried W. Locher wrote that Zwingli believed Jews and heathens were part of the one church. This was a "pet doctrine" for Zwingli.[18]

In 1531, after the publication of the catechisms, Zwingli went even further in his radical opinion:

> Then they [you] may hope to see the whole company and assemblage of all the saints, the wise, the faithful, brave, and good who have lived since the world began. . . . Hercules, Theseus, Socrates, Aristidies, Antigonus, Numa, Camillus, the Catos and Scipios. . . . In short there has not been a good man and will not be a holy heart or faithful soul from the beginning of the world to the end thereof that you will not see in heaven with God. (*Exposition of the Christian Faith*)[19]

Philip Schaff explained in *The Creeds of Christendom*,

> [Zwingli] believed also in the salvation of those heathen who loved truth and righteousness in this life, and were, so to say, unconscious Christians, or pre-Christian Christians. This is closely connected with his humanistic liberalism and enthusiasm for the ancient classics. He admired the wisdom and virtue of the Greeks and Romans, and expected to meet in heaven, not only the saints of the Old Testament from Adam down to John the Baptist, but also such men as Socrates, Plato, Pindar, Aristides, Numa, Cato,

Scipio, Seneca; yea, even such mythical characters as Hercules and Theseus. There is, he says, no good and holy man, no faithful soul, from the beginning to the end of the world, that shall not see God in his glory.[20]

Take note! To illustrate Luther's full rejection of Zwingli's doctrine, Schaff cited LC II 66![21] As will be shown in Chapter 6, the argument in LC II 66 directly opposes the doctrine of the pious heathen as described by Zwingli.

In the years after the publication of the catechisms, Luther specifically mentioned and rejected Zwingli's teachings about natural and philosophical knowledge of God.

> Zwingli wrote some time ago that Numa Pompilius, Hector, Scipio, and Hercules are enjoying eternal blessedness in Paradise along with Peter, Paul, and all the other saints. This is nothing else than an open acknowledgement that they think that faith and Christianity amount to nothing. For if Scipio and Numa Pompilius, who were idolaters, have been saved, why was it necessary for Christ to suffer and die, and to what end is it necessary for Christians to be baptized and for Christ to be taught? So horribly do men fall when the Word has been neglected and laid aside, and they know nothing about faith, but set up and teach that very thing, namely, "that a man who does what is in him is saved" [*Homo faciens, quod in se est, salvatur*].[22]

Note well how Luther equated Zwingli's opinion with the scholastic doctrine that a person could "do that which was in him" (*facere quod in se est*) and attain faith and grace. Luther seems unaware of Zwingli's basis for the doctrine about the pious heathen in predestination. Schaff wrote, "The great and good Luther was horrified at the idea that even 'the godless Numa' (!) [an idolater] should be saved, and thought that it falsified the whole gospel, without which there can be no salvation."[23] Luther ultimately regarded Zwingli with contempt and at times called him a heathen.[24] It seems likely that Luther had Zwingli or other disciples of humanism in mind when he wrote LC II 63–70.

CONCLUSION

Luther was fully familiar with the scholastic doctrine that a person could attain "acquired faith" by natural knowledge and human strength. He also learned of the doctrine about the pious heathen, which taught that a person could believe in and worship the one true God without knowing Christ. (It is not clear when Luther learned about this doctrine.) In LC II 66, Luther was not presenting an abstract argument but had a specific doctrine in view. He had combated and rejected the scholastic doctrine already in 1518. In the late 1520s, he was wrestling with opinions of Erasmus and Zwingli. For these reasons, it is likely that in LC II 63–70 Luther was arguing against the doctrines of Erasmus or the Swiss Reformers rather than the scholastics.

NOTES

1. See AE 25 for Luther's careful glosses and scholia on Romans 1:20–21 (e.g., first quote under "Pagans and Philosophers" in Chapter 5). Regarding the Heidelberg Disputations, Heino O. Kadai wrote, "In Thesis 19 Luther speaks primarily to scholastic theologians when he warns that true theologians should know better than to try to speculate about God on the basis of created world and historical data." "Luther's Theology of the Cross," in *Accents in Luther's Theology* (St. Louis: CPH, 1967), 241.
2. A similar idea is expressed in English as "just do your best and everything will be fine."
3. This is the technical term in modern literature. It is not clear that Zwingli used these specific terms to describe his teaching.
4. See W. P. Stephens, *The Theology of Huldrych Zwingli* (Oxford: Clarendon Press, 1986), 124–27. G. C. A. Harless lists the scholastic theologian Abelard and the Swiss theologians Zwingli, Bucer, and Bullinger as holding the opinion that God gave faith also to the pious heathen. *Commentar über den Brief Pauli an die Ephesier* (Erlangen: Carl Heyder, 1834), 212. Bibliander may have also held this view. See *The Oxford Dictionary of the Christian Church*, 2nd ed. (Oxford: Oxford University Press, 1983), 173. Martin Chemnitz attributed this opinion to Luther's opponents Latomus (ca. 1490–1570) and Theobald Thamer (1502–69), who studied at Wittenberg but later converted to Romanism. See *Loci Theologici* (St. Louis: CPH, 1989) 1:53–54. Modern Roman Catholicism teaches a similar view: "Those who, through no fault of their own, do not know of the Gospel of Christ or his Church, but who nevertheless seek God with a sincere heart, and, moved by grace, try in their actions to do his will as they know it through the dictates of their conscience—those too may achieve eternal salvation" (*Lumen gentium* 16, cited from *Catechism of the Catholic Church* (Mahwah, NJ: Paulist Press, 1994), §847, p. 224.

5. "[Erasmus] had a high opinion of the morality and piety of the nobler heathen, such as Socrates, Cicero, and Plutarch. 'The Scriptures,' he says in his *Colloquies*, 'deserve, indeed the highest authority; but I find also in the writings of the ancient heathen and in the poets so much that is pure, holy and divine, that I must believe that their hearts were divinely moved. The spirit of Christ is perhaps more widely diffused that we imagine, and many will appear among the saints who are not in our catalogue.' Then after quoting from Cicero and Socrates, he says, 'I can often hardly restrain myself from exclaiming, 'Holy Socrates, pray for us.' The same liberal sentiments we find among the early Greek fathers (Justin Martyr, Clement of Alexandria, Origen), and in Zwingli." Schaff, *History of the Christian Church*, VII:414. "That Zwingli never got rid entirely of the Erasmian ideas is also evident from the fact that shortly before his death, in his *Christianae Fidei Exposito*, he ranks Hercules, Theseus, Socrates, Aristides, Numa, *et al.*, with the saints of the Old and New Testaments, with Isaiah and Elijah, with Peter and Paul, among the saints in heaven (St. L. XX:1767)." Francis Pieper, *Christian Dogmatics* (St. Louis: CPH, 1953), III:167.

6. Ulrich Zwingli, "On Original Sin," in *On Providence and Other Essays* (Durham, NC: The Labyrinth Press, 1983 reprint), 12–13. "Quid enim scimus, quid fidei quisque in corde suo dei manu scriptum teneat? Sencae viri sanctissimi fidem, quam epistola ad Lucilium 34. prodit, . . . Quis, quaeso, hanc fidem in cor hominis huius scripsit? Neque quisquam putet ista in evacuationem Christi tendre, ut quidam nos insimulant; amplificant enim illius gloriam." *Corpus Reformatorum* (Halis Saxonum: C.A. Schetschke, 1834–1860), XCII:379.

7. Gottfried W. Locher, *Die Seligkeit erwählter Heiden bei Zwingli* (Zollikon, 1952).

8. Throughout the next few years Luther's letters are filled with references to Zwingli and the Swiss theologians who actively attacked Luther's teachings on the Lord's Supper and tried to draw pastors away from Luther. The battleground was Strassburg and southern Germany. Luther frequently asked his friends for prayer as he expressed his anger and disappointment over the Swiss. He titled them "the Sacramentarians" because of their false teaching about the Sacrament. But there are many other colorful descriptions. (They had a swarming spirit, were examples of God's wrath, were vain, and were attackers for Satan, rude, poorly educated, boastful, triumphal, and imperious; they were hinderers of the Gospel and rabid pests.) In the letters from the summer of 1528, the references fade away and Luther focused more on the issue of the visitation of the churches in Saxony, the experience that would compel him to write the catechisms. In the same year that Luther finished the catechisms (March and April 1529), he met with the Swiss at the Marburg Colloquy (October), where they could not come to full agreement. In his letters from the late 1520s, Luther also mentioned Erasmus, the Anabaptists, Henry VIII, and other opponents. But they do not appear nearly as often as the Swiss. For example, even though Erasmus published a major treatise against Luther at this time, Luther hardly noticed and never responded. Other opponents bothered Luther. The Swiss theologians truly concerned him.

9. See AE 37:15n 7.

10. AE 37:16, 53.

11. See G. R. Potter, *Zwingli* (Cambridge: Cambridge University Press, 1976), 310. See also AE 37:16n7; AE 37:53–54. Based on the theological discussions before the

Marburg Colloquy (October 1, 1529), Philipp Melanchthon also listed a number of issues. He described this in a letter shortly after the colloquy: "Zwingli, for instance, has written that there is no original sin, but that sin consists only of outward evil works and actions, while original sin denotes only innate impurity and lusts of the heart. He also teaches that it is not sin if by nature we do not fear God and believe [glauben] in him. This indicates clearly that Zwingli does not know much about true Christian holiness, because he finds sin in outward deeds only, like the Pelagians and all papists and philosophers. . . . We have learned that some of them [the Swiss] speak about the Godhead as the Jews do, as if Christ were not true, essential God [natürlicher Gott]." This is likely a reference to Zwingli's treatise *On Original Sin* (1526). Cf. Luther's comments on holiness at LC II 56. Hermann Sasse, *This Is My Body* (Adelaide: Lutheran Publishing House, 1959), 181. See CR I:1099.

12. See Gottfried W. Locher, *Zwingli's Thought: New Perspectives* (Leiden: E. J. Brill, 1981), 54–56.

13. "In the times of the Reformation Universalists were found among Anabaptists, Lollards, and Protestant mystics." George T. Knight, *The New Schaff-Herzog Encyclopedia of Religious Knowledge*, ed. S. M. Jackson (Grand Rapids: Baker, 1950), XII:96. In AE 37:372 Luther wrote in passing, "I do not agree with those who teach that the devils also will finally be restored to salvation." This refers to the universalism of some early Christian theologians (e.g., Origen).

14. Gottfried W. Locher, *Die Theoligie Huldriych Zwinglis*, 55.

15. I provide the following summaries from LC II for the reader's convenience.

16. Potter, *Zwingli*, 296.

17. Schaff, *History of the Christian Church* VII:620–29.

18. *Die Theologie Huldriych Zwinglis in Lichte seiner Christologie. Erster Teil: Die Gotteslehre* (Zurich: Zwingli-Verlag, 1952), 31.

19. Zwingli, 271–72. "Deinde sperandum est tibi visurum esse sanctorum, pruden-tium, fidelium, constantium, fortium, virtuosorum omnium, quicunque a con-dito mundo fuerunt, sodalitatem, coetum et contuberium. . . hic Herculum, Theseum, Socratem, Aristidem; Antigonum, Numam, Camillum, Catones, Scipiones; . . . Et summatim: non fuit vir bonus, nonent mens sancta, nos est fidelis anima ab ipso mundi exordio usque ad eius consummationem, quem non sis ist hic cum deo visurus." CR XCII:131–32.

20. Schaff, *History of the Christian Church*, VIII:95. In fn. 3 he adds, "[Zwingli] often speaks on this subject in his epistles, commentaries, the tract on Providence, and most confidently at the close of his *Exposition of the Christian Faith*, addressed to the king of France." *On Providence* (1530) and the *Exposition of the Christian Faith* (1531) were written after Luther wrote the Large Catechism. However, as Schaff notes, Zwingli had often spoken of this subject in letters and commentaries.

21. Philip Schaff , *The Creeds of Christendom*, 6th ed. (Grand Rapids: Baker, 1990), I:382n2.

22. Luther's comments were prompted by the posthumous publication of Zwingli's *Exposition of the Christian Faith* in 1531. At that time Bucer angered Luther by elaborating on Zwingli's doctrine of the pious heathen. See Hastings Eells, *Martin Bucer* (New Haven: Yale, 1931), 472n43; Gustav Anrich, *Martin Bucer* (Strassburg:

Karl J. Trübner, 1914), 123–24. AE 8:134; see *Luthers Werke* (Weimar: Hermann Böhlau, 1912), 44:677. See also AE 26:173–76. Luther specifically mentioned that the Sacramentarians (i.e., Zwingli, etc.) rejected the doctrine of "Christian righteousness" through faith in Christ.

23. Schaff, *The Creeds of Christendom*, I:382.
24. Schaff, *History of the Christian Church*, VIII:177n1.

Chapter 5

THE NATURAL
KNOWLEDGE OF GOD

*Reason never finds the true God, but it finds the devil or its
own concept of God, ruled by the devil. So there is a vast difference between knowing that there is a God and knowing
who or what God is. Nature knows the former—it is
inscribed in everybody's heart; the latter is taught only by the
Holy Spirit.*[1]

—Martin Luther, Commentary on Jonah, AE 19

This chapter will draw together quotes from Luther about what
people from other religions know about the one true God (based
on the various groups he listed in LC II 66b). These quotations will
illustrate what Luther stated in LC II 63b and will also show that passage's importance for Luther's argument in LC II 66.

GENERAL STATEMENT

I have often said that the confidence and faith [*Glaube*] of
the heart alone make both God and an idol. If your faith
[*Glaube*] and trust be right, then is your god also true; and,
on the other hand, if your trust be false and wrong, then

you do not have the true God; for these two belong together, faith [*Glaube*] and God. (LC I 3; 1529)

Luther distinguished between genuine faith in God and false faith in a god or gods. He did not believe it was possible to have genuine faith and a false god or to have false faith and the true God. His conclusions were based on Romans 1:21–23.

PAGANS AND PHILOSOPHERS

They confess it also by works, by calling upon him, worshiping and adoring him of whom they think that divinity resides in him . . . they changed the truth of God into a lie. Thus they knew that the nature of divinity, or of God, is that He is powerful, invisible, just immortal and good. They know the invisible things of God, His eternal power and divinity. This major premise of the "practical syllogism," this theological "insight of the conscience," is in all men and cannot be obscured. But in the minor premise they erred when they said and claimed: "Now, this one," that is, Jupiter or any other who is like this image, "is of this type, etc." . . . If they had stayed with this feeling and had said: "Look, we know this: Whoever this God, or this Divinity . . . let us worship and adore Him, let us not call Him Jupiter and say that He is like this or that image, but let us simply worship Him, no matter who He is (for He must have being)," then without doubt they would have been saved, even though they had not recognized Him as the Creator of heaven and earth or taken note of any other specific work of His hands. (AE 25:157–58; 1515)

Even if natural reason in itself is not concerned with spiritual truth or divine activity, nevertheless, when it asserts affirmative statements (to use their jargon) its judgment is wrong, but when it asserts negative statements its judgment is right. Reason does not comprehend what God is, but it most certainly comprehends what God is not. (AE 44:336; 1521)

Nature provides that we should call [*anruffen*] upon God. The Gentiles attest to this fact. For there never was a Gentile who did not call upon his idols, even though these were not the true God [*rechten Gottes*]. (AE 35:168; 1525)

Let us here learn from nature and from reason what can be known of God. These people regard God as a being who is able to deliver from every evil. It follows from this that natural reason must concede that all that is good comes from God . . . It regards God as kind, gracious, merciful, and benevolent. And that is indeed a bright light. . . . But they do not believe that God is disposed to help them. . . . This situation calls for a faith [*glaube*] that does not doubt but is convinced that God wants to be gracious not only to others but also to me. That is genuine and a live faith [*rechter, lebendiger glaube*]; it is a great and rich and rare gift of the Holy Spirit, and so we shall see it in Jonah. . . . Reason is unable to identify God properly; it cannot ascribe the Godhead to the One who is entitled to it exclusively. It knows that there is a God, but it does not know who or which is the true God. . . . Reason never finds the true God, but it finds the devil or its own concept of God, ruled by the devil. So there is a vast difference between knowing that there is a God and knowing who or what God is. Nature knows the former—it is inscribed in everybody's heart; the latter is taught only by the Holy Spirit. (AE 19:54–55; 1526)

Those who maintain that the natural endowments have remained unimpaired surely do not see how much we have lost. For the will that is good and righteous, that pleases God, obeys God, trusts in the Creator, and makes use of the creatures with an expression of thanks has been lost to such an extent that our will makes a devil out of God and shudders at the mention of His name, especially when it is troubled by God's judgment. (AE 1:142; 1535)

Philosophers argue and ask speculative questions about God and arrive at some kind of knowledge. . . . But everything is merely objective; it is not yet that knowledge which Joseph has, that God cares, that He hears that afflicted and helps them. (AE 8:17; 1545)

Note well how Luther believed that natural knowledge of God exists; that is, mankind naturally senses and concludes that there is a God (cf. Rom 1:20). However, Luther undermined the view that people arrive at natural knowledge of God by their own reason. Such knowledge is an inherent quality of being human, like having a God-given sense of right and wrong. Also, Luther does not at all allow that the knowledge of God's existence is the same as knowing and believing in the one true God. Because mankind is corrupt, people naturally corrupt their knowledge of God into idolatry (cf. Rom 1:21–23). As a consequence, all people outside of Christianity do not have genuine faith and worship—they are idolaters—for they create a god of their own imagination apart from Scripture and Christ.

MONOTHEISTS

Allah means God, and is a corruption of the Hebrew *Eloha*. For they have been taught in the Koran that they shall boast constantly with these words, "There is no God but God." All that is really a device of the devil. For what does it mean to say, "There is no God but God," without distinguishing one God from another? The devil, too, is a god, and they honor him with this word; there is no doubt of that. (AE 46:183; 1528)

The Turk says he adores [*adorare*] the God who made heaven and earth . . . the Jew says the same. But because both deny that this King is the Son of God, they not only wander away from God, but also adore an idol of their own heart. For they invent a god such as they wish to have, not as God has revealed Himself. But God detests them and closes His ears to their prayers. For He wishes to hear and see no one except through His Son. (AE 12:84; 1532)

The faith [*glaub*] of the Jews and the Turks is nothing but sheer blindness, for they exclude the Son and want to retain only the Father. This is the chief article of our Christian faith: that the Son is eternal and true God [*wahr hafftiger Gott*], and also true man, sent into the world for its salvation. This article annuls the belief [*glauben*] of the Jews, the Turks, and all others who renounce the Son and thus worship [*anbeten*] another god and look to another source for help. The Turk is not able to pray the Lord's Prayer or the articles of the Creed. Faith [*gleuben*], to which God alone is entitled, is the chief type of worship [*Gottesdienst*]. (AE 22:392–93; ca. 1537)

It is no avail to Jews, Turks, and heretics to feign great religious zeal and to boast against us Christians of their belief in one God, the Creator of heaven and earth, and that they devoutly call Him Father. These are nothing but inane and empty words with which they take the name of God in vain and misuse it contrary to the Second Commandment. . . . Here you can note that they do not know what God is. When they speak of God, Creator and Father, they do not know what they are saying. . . . Consequently they have no God, except that they sinfully and shamefully misuse the name of God and fabricate their own god as creator, who is to be their father and they his children. (AE 15:314; 1543)

At the same time Luther was writing the Large Catechism, he was writing "On War against the Turk," the first document quoted in this section. It shows markedly that Luther regarded Allah as a false god— the devil—not to be equated with the one true God. The remaining quotes illustrate the consistency of Luther's belief on this topic.

FALSE CHRISTIANS AND HYPOCRITES

The core is this: that without any merit, as a gift of God's pure grace in Christ, we attain righteousness, life, and salvation, and that there is no other way or path, no other means or effort, that can help us attain it. . . . If this one teaching stands in its purity, then Christendom will also remain pure and good, undivided and unseparated;

for this alone, and nothing else, makes and maintains Christendom. Everything else may be brilliantly counterfeited by false Christians and hypocrites. (AE 14: 36–37; 1530)

"False Christians" refers to heretics. "Hypocrites" is another kind of false Christian. Luther did not use the term "hypocrites" as we do to describe genuine Christians who stumble in their faith. He meant outwardly Christian groups that held they were justified by works rather than by God's grace in Christ (e.g., Smalcald Articles (SA) III II 18; III III 27; see also Melanchthon's usage in the Apology of the Augsburg Confession (Ap) IV 20–21; V 200; VII/VIII 3, 12, 28; XXIII 46).

CONCLUSION

The quotations from Luther clearly demonstrate that he believed "all outside of Christianity"—including those who profess monotheism and those who falsely professed Christianity—believed in and worshipped a false god and not the one true God. His theology is very consistent on this topic.

NOTE

1. Luther emphasized that the Holy Spirit worked through the Word, through the means of grace administered by the Church. Zwingli emphasized that the Holy Spirit could and did work without the means of grace; special revelation to the heathen was not tied to the Word. For Zwingli, the "church" naturally included those who were not Christians. See Locher, *Die Theologie Huldriych Zwinglis in Lichte seiner Christologie*, 56–57.

Chapter 6

LUTHER'S ARGUMENTS "FROM THE IMPOSSIBLE"

St. Paul here names the parts [of the argument] one after the other and arrays them per impossible, as I said.

—Martin Luther, AE 28:100

This chapter will describe Luther's use of dialectic in LC II 63–66b. The term *dialectic* comes from διαλέγεσθαι, which means "to discuss."[1] It started as reasoning that "proceeded by question and answer."[2] Luther and other students of the late medieval period were trained in dialectic at an early age. The textbooks for dialectic were based primarily on the writings of Aristotle.

Luther's rejection of Aristotle and his break with late medieval scholasticism are well known from his *Disputation Against Scholastic Theology* (1519).[3] Although Luther rejected the gross abuse of speculative dialectical arguments, he never stopped using his education in dialectic for presenting theology, defending the Gospel, and expounding Scripture. He regarded such training as basic since it was rooted in common sense.[4] For example, in 1521 the Louvain scholastic theologian Latomus published an attack on Luther's teachings. Luther responded in part by pointing out deficiencies in Latomus's dialectical arguments:

I would like to be given one of his pupils who had even for a day heard lectures on dialectic, so that I might examine him on the skill of his teacher. Tell me, boy, is it true, as the first principles of Aristotle would have it, that all those inferences are valid which presuppose that anything follows from the impossible? For instance, does this properly follow from the rule that anything may be inferred from the impossible: three and two equal eight, therefore the devil is God? Now as soon as the antecedent is true, the consequence also is true.[5]

Luther continued mocking this way for several pages, complaining that Latomus "cannot even grasp ordinary common sense nor the rudiments of a schoolboy's learning."

ARGUMENTS FROM THE IMPOSSIBLE

In the statement against Latomus, Luther mentioned arguing points "from the impossible." This refers to one of the basic principles of dialectic known as *reductio ad impossibile*, which may have been among the first things students learned.[6] This basic form of argument actually predated Aristotle, who attributed it to Zeno of Elea (ca. 470 BC). Aristotle refers to *per impossibile* arguments frequently in the Prior Analytics.

> What Aristotle attributed to Zeno was presumably the discovery of the use of the *reductio ad impossibile* in metaphysics, and it is possible that this was suggested to Zeno himself by its use in Pythagorean mathematics. . . . It seems, then, that the first precise meaning of the word "dialectic" was *reductio ad impossibile* in metaphysics.[7]

The Greek term is απαγωγη εις το αδύνατον (literally, an argument "leading to the impossible"). It was adopted by Latin scholars and commonly used by the scholastics and those trained in their tradition.[8]

The *reductio ad impossibile* technique tests the truth of statements by measuring them against known facts. For example, someone may assert, "Water freezes." To test this *per impossibile*, one may turn the statement into a concession that states the opposite of the original statement. Then one draws inferences: If (*per impossibile*) water does not freeze, then ice does not exist. However, since ice does exist, the original proposition "water freezes" is true.[9]

Arguments *per impossibile* have a distinct grammatical form. They always include (1) a conditional, concessive clause and (2) a conclusion.[10] In most cases the sentence is structured in a concession-conclusion format, though other forms can be used (see Appendix B). This definite sentence structure for *per impossibile* arguments, which Luther used frequently, will be considered further in the chapters on grammar. However, take note here of the close relationship between this type of argument and grammatical structure. As one linguist wrote, "An elaborate inventory of concessive expressions, as found in European languages, presupposes, it seems, a certain tradition of argumentative writing."[11] Also, as modern logicians have stated, "Logic and language, the proposition and the sentence, are intimately connected."[12] The structure of this formal, logical argument had been well established for centuries before Luther studied it in his coursework.

Luther frequently used the *per impossibile* method of reasoning.[13] To make the steps of this reasoning clearer, we will walk through five different examples of such arguments from Luther's writings. The first three examples are passages from the Large Catechism and the Smalcald Articles (SA) (drawn from Appendix D). The fourth example is from Luther's commentary on St. Paul and does not include the explicit term *per impossibile*. (Note well: in most cases dialecticians do not include the technical term in their argument but rely on the reader to understand the argument based on structure and content.) The last example treated will be LC II 66. In each case the steps of dialectical analysis are spelled out. Luther would not have needed this step-by-step process, since his training would have allowed him to go directly from the proposition to the *per impossibile* argument.

EXAMPLE 1 (*TRIGLOTTA*, LC Preface 9)

In Luther's day, lazy people were asserting the following proposition:

People know and understand the Catechism well enough.

Luther disagreed with this proposition. So, he turned it into a more intense proposition, which he viewed as impossible:

> They should know and understand the Catechism perfectly.

He then drew an inference (a conclusion) to test the proposition:

> Even if they knew the Catechism perfectly, there are still manifold benefits and fruits to be obtained by reading it daily and practicing it in thought and speech.

Luther's conclusion cancels out the original proposition, showing that people can't know the Catechism well enough. In the Large Catechism he wrote this *per impossibile* argument as follows:

> For though they should know and understand it perfectly (*which, however, is impossible in this life*), yet there are manifold benefits and fruits still to be obtained, if it be daily read and practised in thought and speech. (*Triglotta*, LC Preface 9; emphasis added)[14]

EXAMPLE 2 (*TRIGLOTTA*, LC IV 55)

Anabaptists were asserting the following proposition:

> Infants cannot believe, so those baptized as infants should be rebaptized.

Luther took this proposition and turned it into a concession that he regarded as impossible:

> Suppose I grant that infants do not believe.

He then drew an inference (conclusion) to test the original proposition:

> The infants' Baptism would still be valid because of God's Word and promise and no one should rebaptize them.

Luther's conclusion cancels out the original proposition, showing that the validity of the Sacrament of Baptism does not ultimately depend upon our faith. In the Large Catechism, he wrote this *per impossibile* argument as follows:

> For (as we have said) even though infants did not believe, *which, however, is not the case,* yet their baptism as now shown would be valid, and no one should rebaptize them. (*Triglotta*, LC IV 55; emphasis added)[15]

EXAMPLE 3 (*TRIGLOTTA*, SA II IV 7)

In this third example, Luther uses a *per impossibile* argument to point out a shortcoming in his own reasoning. During the Reformation, Luther and his colleagues were asserting the following proposition:

> The papacy is of no use in the Church.

Luther knew the papacy disagreed with this proposition. He even had second thoughts about it himself. So, he took this proposition and turned it into a concession that he regarded as impossible:

> Suppose that the Pope and See at Rome would accept this and resign.

He then drew an inference (a conclusion) to test the proposition:

> Christianity would not be helped, but many more sects would arise than before.

Luther's conclusion undermined his original proposition. He acknowledged that the papacy did serve at least one useful function: it helped to curb the number of sects that might arise in Christianity. In the Smalcald Articles, he wrote this *per impossibile* argument as follows:

> Supposing, I say, that the Pope and See at Rome would yield and accept this [idea that they were of no use] (*which, nevertheless, is impossible . . .*), even in this way Christianity would not be helped, but many more sects would arise than before. (*Triglotta*, SA II IV 7; emphasis added)[16]

EXAMPLE 4 (LUTHER BIBEL, 1 CORINTHIANS 15:13)

The first three examples were based on *per impossibile* statements that explicitly included wording to show that the concession was impossible. As stated, most *per impossibile* arguments do not include such wording. They depend on the context and understanding of the reader to conclude that their concessions are contrary to fact and simply part of the argument.[17] To illustrate this, here is an example from St. Paul's first epistle to the Corinthians. Someone at Corinth was asserting the following:

> There is no resurrection of the dead.

Paul disagreed with this proposition, so he turned it into a concession that he regarded as impossible:

> Suppose there is no resurrection of the dead.

He then drew an inference (a conclusion) to test the proposition:

> Then, Christ is not raised from the dead.

Paul's inference cannot be true. As a result, the original proposition cannot be true. Paul wrote his *per impossibile* argument as follows:

> If there is no resurrection of the dead, then Christ also is not raised. (1 Cor 15:13)[18]

Luther described this very passage as an example of *per impossibile* reasoning, even though the apostle never indicated that his concession is an argument from the impossible.[19]

> He makes proper use of that device of dialectics which is known as *reducere per impossible*. He wants to say: "Whoever denies this article must simultaneously deny far more, namely first of all, that you believe properly; in the second place, that the Word which you believe has been true; in the third place, that we apostles preach correctly and that we are God's apostles; in the fourth place, that God is truthful; in brief, that God is God. . . . St. Paul here names

the parts one after the other and arrays them *per impossible*, as I said.[20]

This passage proves that Luther was fully acquainted with this dialectical argument and recognized its common form and usage.

THE ARGUMENT IN LC II 66B

In LC II 63–66, Luther was considering a line of reasoning regarding natural knowledge of God. As stated above, arguments about "natural theology" based on "natural reason" were used by some scholastics and some Reformers, who were intent on building a connection between natural philosophy and theology. Luther began by stating his own proposition in LC II 63b when he wrote,

> For although the whole world with all diligence has endeavored to ascertain what God is, what He has in mind and does, yet has she never been able to attain to [knowledge and understanding of] any of these things.[21]

In LC II 66b Luther took up the opponent's proposition, which can be summarized as follows:

> Some people outside Christianity believe in and worship the one true God.[22]

Since Luther disagreed with this proposition, he sought to undermine it. He first turned the proposition into a universal statement, putting the argument into its most extreme and generous form:

> Suppose all outside of Christianity believe in and worship only one true God.

Then Luther noted that even this most generous form of the proposition could not help unbelievers because those outside of Christianity (1) do not know God's mind toward them, (2) cannot expect any love or blessings from Him, (3) do not have the Lord Christ, and (4) are not illumined or favored with any gifts of the Holy Spirit. Here is the full argument as Luther presented it:

> For all outside of Christianity, . . . although they believe in and worship, only one true God, yet know not what His mind toward them is, and cannot expect any love or blessing from Him; therefore they abide in eternal wrath and damnation. For they have not the Lord Christ, and, besides, they are not illumined and favored by any gifts of the Holy Ghost. (*Triglotta*, LC II 66)[23]

Luther's argumentation and sentence structure here conform with his *per impossibile* arguments in other places and with the history of this dialectical argument. His training in grammar and dialectic manifest themselves clearly in the passage. More will be noted about this in the grammar section on concessive conditional clauses.

CONCLUSION

Luther knew and frequently used *per impossibile* arguments. The structure and content of LC II 63–66 are in *per impossibile* form. For this reason the controversial clause in LC II 66b is a proposition that Luther was conceding for the sake of his argument. It is not a statement of his doctrine.

NOTES

1. William and Martha Kneale, *The Development of Logic* (Oxford: Clarendon Press, 1975), 7.
2. Ted Honderich, ed., *The Oxford Companion to Philosophy* (Oxford: Oxford University Press, 1995). This method of reasoning and teaching should sound familiar, since catechesis also proceeded by: question, answer, discussion.
3. AE 31:9–16.
4. "Dialectica is a profitable and necessary art, which justly ought to be studied and learned; it shows how we ought to speak orderly and uprightly, what we should acknowledge and judge to be right or wrong; 'tis not only necessary in schools, but also in consistories, in courts of justice, and in churches; in churches most especially." *The Table Talk of Martin Luther*, ed. Thomas S. Kepler (Grand Rapids: Baker, 1952), 498. See WA, Tischreden 6244. Note how Luther described dialectic as showing one "how to speak orderly and uprightly," illustrating the overlap between dialectic and rhetoric. The disciplines were studied together and viewed as fully complimentary.
5. AE 32:185.

6. This is a different name for reductio ad absurdum, which Luther also used. See Concordia Theological Seminary, "Opinion of the Department of Systematic Theology: The Fruit of the Vine in the Sacrament of the Altar," Concordia *Theological Quarterly* 45, nos. 1–2 (January–April 1981), 79.

7. Kneale, *The Development of Logic*, 8–9.

8. James F. Ross and Todd Bates provide a helpful example in "Duns Scotus on Natural Theology" in *The Cambridge Companion to Duns Scotus*, ed. Thomas Williams (Cambridge: Cambridge University Press, 2003), 194. "Scotus characteristically and deftly argues by *indirect proof*. He supposes the opposite of his intended conclusion and deduces a contradiction between that supposition and certain self-evident or previously proved propositions, thus getting his own conclusion by using the principle that whatever entails the denial of what is already known to be so is false and its opposite true: "si negatur negatio, ponitur affirmatio." He also uses the argument form "if 'p' is not necessary, then 'not-p' is possible." And he uses the general rule "if possibly P, and not contingently P, then necessarily P" as well as the rule that "whatever is possible is necessarily possible." "Indirect proof" is the modern term for the classical *reductio ad impossibile*.

9. Melanchthon wrote, "Duo modi reductionis traduntur. . . . Alter modus, *reductio per impossibile* [emphasis added], rerum confirmatio est. Cum enim ostеditur una contradictoria esse impossibilis, alterum verum esse necessario sequitur. . . . Immo et in Rhetoricis contrariorum collectione multa illustrantur." *Corpus Reformatorum* XIII:613. He has a section on "Ab impossibili" on p. 689, which is a related form of argument. Melanchthon first wrote his *Dialectica* in 1520 and revised it twice. See CR XIII:507–10.

10. To state this dialectically, they include (1) a proposition and (2) inferences.

11. Ekkehard König, "Concessive Connectives and Concessive Sentences: Cross-Linguistic Regularities and Pragmatic Principles," in *Explaining Language Universals*, ed. John A. Hawkins (Oxford: Basil Blackwell Ltd., 1988), 145.

12. Albert Myrton Frye and Albert William Levi, *Rational Belief: An Introduction to Logic* (New York: Harcourt, Brace and Company, 1941), 158.

13. Appendix B presents fourteen explicit examples of this technique, where Luther included the term *per impossibile* (or a German equivalent) as he would in school exercises.

14. "Denn ob sie es gleich allerdings aufs allerbeste wüszten und könnten (das doch nicht möglich ist in diesem Leben), so ist doch mancherlei Nutz und Frucht dahinten, so man's täglich liest und übt mit Gedanken und Reden." (*Triglotta*, 568). The Latin text is also interesting because the translator renders this concessive clause with an ACI (accusative with infinitive) construction. This grammar is also found in the Latin translation of LC II 66b. See also p. 73.

15. "Denn (wie gesagt), wenngleich die Kinder nicht glaubten, welches doch nicht ist, als jetzt beweiset [bewiesen], so wäre doch die Taufe recht und soll sie niemand wieder taufen" (*Triglotta*, 744).

16. "Ich setze nun, sage ich, dasz sich der Papst und der Stuhl zu Rom solches begeben und annehmen wollte (welches doch unmöglich ist . . .), dennoch wäre damit der Christenheit nichts geholfen, und würden viel mehr Rotten werden denn zuvor" (*Triglotta*, 472).

17. This is the common practice in textbooks on logic.
18. "Ist aber die aufferstehung der Todten nichts, so ist auch Christus nicht auffer-standen." (WA, Die Deutsche Bibel, vol. 7:131.) Other verses following are also in *per impossibile* format. See AE 28:95, 100.
19. This passage is also significant grammatically because it uses indicative mood verbs in the concession. The implications of this will be explained further in the grammar section of the book.
20. AE 28:95, 100. This is commentary on 1 Corinthians 15:12–19.
21. "Denn alle Welt, wiewohl sie mit allem Fleisz dannach getrachtet hat, was soch Gott wäre, und was er im Sinn hätte und täte, so hat sie doch der keines je erlan-gen mögen [können]" (*Triglotta*, 694; the Latin includes "*intelligentia aut ratione*").
22. Please note that this proposition is essentially that argued by Zwingli.
23. "Denn was auszer der Christenheit ist, es seien Heiden, Türken, Juden oder falsche Christen und Heuchler, ob sie gleich nur einen wahrhaftigen Gott glauben und anbeten, so wissen sie doch nicht, was er gegen ihnen [wie er gegen sie] gesinnt ist, können sich auch keiner Liebe noch Gutes zu ihm versehen." (*Triglotta*, 694, 696).

Chapter 7

LUTHER'S ALL OR NOTHING STYLE

Rhetoric, which is useful for exhorting, often plays games and often hands you a piece of wood which you suppose is a sword. But dialectic carries on war and busies itself with matters that are serious. Therefore it does not show the opponent pieces of wood; it shows iron.

—Martin Luther, AE 3:191

This chapter will introduce further points about Luther's use of dialectic and rhetoric in LC II 63–66. Luther would have begun study of rhetoric—the art of persuasion—at an early age, since it was part of the medieval trivium of education (grammar, rhetoric, and dialectic). The rhetorical texts of Herennius, Cicero, and Aristotle were commonly taught in medieval schools.[1] Luther likely studied one or more of these texts. His frequent references to Cicero demonstrate clear knowledge of this great Roman orator's style as Melanchthon, a teacher of rhetoric, acknowledged.[2]

While a monk, Luther studied and took notes on Augustine's *De Doctrina Christiana* Book 4, which applied rhetoric to Christianity.[3] Luther would have gained some familiarity with Quintilian's education program in rhetoric (rediscovered in 1416).[4] This is because Quintilian's works were introduced at the University of Wittenberg in 1518 while Luther was a professor.[5] Luther had also read Lorenzo Valla (ca. 1406–57), the great humanist orator and professor of eloquence at Rome.[6]

As the second topic of the medieval trivium, rhetoric was the bridge between grammar and dialectic, applying these topics through exercises in composition and disputation. Disputation was especially important for Luther's early years as a theology student. According to James J. Murphy,

> Apparently every medieval university student underwent some form of the disputation process [*disputatio*], either as an integral part of his classroom work, or as a form of examination. A university teacher of theology, by definition, was a master of disputation.[7]

Rhetorical disputations on theology form an important part of Luther's earliest theological writings. Although Luther's style grew and changed over the years, his education in rhetoric had a lasting influence. He continued to use his skills in rhetoric to shape his own arguments and to critique the arguments of others.[8] Because of the importance of rhetoric for Luther, the rhetorical and dialectical features of LC II 63–66 deserve special consideration.

LUTHER'S USE OF ALL-INCLUSIVE AND EXCLUSIVE TERMS

A notable feature of Luther's rhetoric and dialectic is his love for all-inclusive and exclusive terms. Such terms may be easily overlooked by a modern reader. But to a medieval thinker schooled in rhetoric and dialectic, they were gravely important. Students learned the proper use of these terms in dialectical studies of the "square of oppositions," which contrasted statements built on propositions including such terms as "all," "none," "some," and "some not."[9] Behind this study lay the entire medieval philosophical view of universals (all-inclusive categories) and particulars (exclusive or singular categories). The truth or falsehood of syllogisms and arguments depended on these all-inclusive and exclusive terms.[10]

Luther's sensitivity to all-inclusive and exclusive terms is well illustrated by his arguments for the doctrine of justification by grace *alone*, through faith *alone*. For example, when Luther translated Romans 3:28 he included the term "allein," which did not actually appear in the original Greek text (see AE 35:187–89). Luther's observations about Paul's use of exclusive terms (*particularis exclusivae*) became foundational to Reformation theology and were included in the Lutheran Confessions (see Ap IV 73–74; FC Ep III 7; Solid Declaration of the Formula of Concord [SD] III 36).

In LC II 63–66 Luther used a number of these all-inclusive and exclusive terms. Here is the list:

> . . . entire . . . all . . . all . . . whole . . . all . . . never . . . any . . .
> everything . . . everything . . . never . . . except through . . .
> outside . . . nothing . . . nothing . . . all . . . all outside . . .
> only one . . . cannot . . . any . . . any.[11]

In two paragraphs Luther used nineteen all-inclusive or exclusive terms! These terms demonstrate the dialectical and rhetorical force of Luther's arguments in this passage. As noted, Luther's opponent for LC II 66b was arguing mildly that *some* outside of Christianity believe in and worship the one true God (pp. 29–31). Luther pushed the argument to the highest corners of the "square of oppositions," repeatedly reasoning in all-inclusive and exclusive propositions.

LUTHER'S USE OF ABSURD RHETORICAL ARGUMENTS

In "A Rhetorical Biography: An Analysis of Selected Sermons Preached by Martin Luther," Glenn D. Smith described elements of Luther's rhetoric that are likewise helpful for understanding the character and force of LC II 66. Smith noted Luther's uses of both ridicule and logical development in his sermons:[12] "Luther pursued a plan of *repudiation* [emphasis added] of the old theology of works and concomitant doctrines and sought to establish the 'new theology' grounded in Scriptural evidence."[13] Roman Catholic historian Joseph Lortz has characterized Luther's style as follows:

> His words were not spent in a thin flow of idle rhetoric. On
> the contrary, he possessed, too, a quite unusual power of

concentration. He felt the irresistible need to reduce everything to a few basic doctrines, to a single point. . . . He
knew the scholastic distinctions, but had no time for
them. . . . Not only did Luther love superlatives: he raised
them to the level of paradox. He loved paradox—more than
this, it was the life's blood of his theology. There is nothing
astonishing about this statement: it touches the foundation
of Luther's disposition. His love of paradox is not an over-
flow from an accidental mood, not even simply his basic
mental and spiritual attitude. It is part and parcel of the
core of his theology, of his *theologia crucis*, i.e., of a theology in which contradiction itself appears as the very sign of
truth. The accused criminal on the gallows, forsaken by
God is the Son of God.[14]

Luther drove his readers and listeners forcefully. In fact, in the
Table Talk, Luther described himself as "garrulous and rhetorical" in
contrast with Melanchthon, who was concise and discrete in his
arguments.[15]

Luther shunned the "ornate" rhetoric of Erasmus. Though he
could admire such style, he preferred the sharpness of contrast and
absurdity. Erasmus prized witty satire; Luther prized sarcasm, paradox, and humor. In the following passage, Victoria Kahn has contrasted Luther's argument for the bondage of the will with Erasmus's
argument for the freedom of the will:

While Erasmus argued that those biblical passages which
literally deny free will must be interpreted figuratively,
Luther insisted on the literal meaning of Scripture, including those passages in which God commands man to do
good works. He then argued that although the imperative
mode of these commands would seem to imply that we do
indeed have free will, this is not the case; for God commands us only in order to make us realize that we are incapable of obeying Him. The effect is to make us realize our
absolute dependence on God's grace or charity.[16]

Kahn also noted Luther's remark: "But tropes are no use, and there is no avoiding absurdity [*absurditas*]. For it remains absurd [*Absurdum*] (as Reason judges) that a God who is just and good should demand of free choice impossible things [*impossibilia*]" (Kahn, 99; AE 33:173; WA 18:707). For Luther, God Himself enters into these rhetorical arguments demanding what is absurd and impossible in order to show us our *utter* sinfulness and the *absolute* need for His grace, which *alone* is our salvation.

CONCLUSION

In view of these observations, it will not do to read Luther's arguments flatly, as though he were Melanchthon. When Luther grows rhetorical, a reader should anticipate paradox, absurdity, and arguments from impossibility. These are precisely the features used in LC II 63–66.

NOTES

1. Birgit Stolt, *Martin Luthers Rhetorik des Herzens* (Tübingen: Mohr Siebeck, 2000), 42.
2. Martin Brecht, *Martin Luther: His Road to Reformation*, vol. 1, trans. James L. Schaaf (Minneapolis: Fortress, 1985), 43.
3. Stolt, 43–44.
4. James J. Murphy, *Rhetoric in the Middle Ages* (Berkeley: University of California Press, 1974), 357–59. Spitz, *The Renaissance*, I:151.
5. Stolt, 42.
6. He mentions him in the Table Talk, AE 54:XXII. See Stolt, 43.
7. Murphy, 102.
8. For example, Zwingli's notorious *alloeosis* is a rhetorical argument that Luther vigorously attacked and discredited ("Confession Concerning Christ's Supper" AE 37; FC SD VIII 21). See Richard A. Lanham, *A Handlist of Rhetorical Terms*, 2nd ed. (Berkeley: University of California Press, 1991), 7.
9. A diagram of the square of opposition is printed in Melanchthon's text book on dialectic. CR XIII:585. See Appendix C.
10. Cf. Kneale, *The Development of Logic*, 233.
11. ". . . alle . . . allem . . . keines . . . alles . . . allen . . . alles . . . nimmermehr . . . ohne durch . . . auszer . . . nichts . . . nichts . . . nicht . . . allen . . . was auszer . . . nur einen . . . nicht . . . keiner . . . nicht . . . keinen . . ." (*Triglotta*, 694, 696).
12. Glenn D. Smith, "A Rhetorical Biography: An Analysis of Selected Sermons Preached by Martin Luther," (PhD diss., University of Nebraska, August 1971), 206, 209.
13. Smith, 210.

14. *The Reformation in Germany* (New York: Herder and Herder, 1968), I:174. In his characterization of Luther's style, Lortz used terms related to key dialectical terms: "reduce," "superlatives," "paradox," and "contradiction." Luther rejected the scholastic love of subtlety and distinction, of reasoning in formal syllogisms from the bottom of the square of oppositions ("some" or "some not"). Luther pushed the arguments to the top of the square of oppositions, forming all or nothing arguments. He vigorously simplified the reasoning (i.e., he applied Occam's razor: a simpler argument is less likely to contain errors; therefore, a simple argument is more likely to be true). Paradox occurs when two propositions are contradictory, yet both are true. The temptation for a subtle thinker is to subordinate one of the truths in order to resolve the contradiction. Luther simply will not allow this subordination. For example, a Christian is a sinner; a Christian is a saint. Luther will not allow the more complex, subtle argument that some Christians are more saint than they are sinner, or vice versa. Luther is not illogical, as some of his critics charged. He was using a different kind of logic, one rooted in biblical and confessional paradoxes (e.g., Christ is true God and true man in one person) rather than Aristotle's syllogisms. "The scholastic conception of logic was essentially formal. The syllogistic rules were tought [*sic*] to guarantee that the syllogistic form necessarily gives a true conclusion whenever the variables have been replaced by suitable categorematic terms, notwithstanding the matter of terms and propositions. . . . This kind of problematic situation, however, is brought forth when Trinitarian (and Christological) terms are introduced into the discourse. In the syllogisms compiled by them the premises are true, but the conclusions false." Reijo Tyoeinoja, "Proprietas Verbi: Luther's Conception of Philosophical and Theological Language in the Disputation: Verbum caro factum est (Jn 1:14), 1539" in *Faith, Will, and Grammar: Some Themes of Intensional Logic and Semantics in Medieval and Reformation Thought*, ed. Heikki Kirjavainen (Helsinki: Luther-Agricola-Society, 1986), 161. Beneath the argument in LC II 63–66 are the following propositions: all people who are in Christ are saved; all people who are not in Christ are damned. Luther will not allow the subtle argument that some people who have not heard of Christ are saved through Christ (this is Zwingli's argument).

15. AE 54:440. See also F. Bente, *Historical Introductions to the Lutheran Confessions*, 2nd ed. (St. Louis: CPH, 2005), who describes Melanchthon's "Pussy footing" (Leisetreten), pp. 38, 41–43, 77.

16. Victoria Kahn, *Rhetoric, Prudence, and Skepticism in the Renaissance* (Ithaca: Cornell University Press, 1985), 84. Take note: Kahn summarized Luther's argument with a sentence in *per impossibile* form (second sentence in the quote). She has adopted Luther's style in order to describe his rhetoric and dialectic.

Chapter 8

CONCESSIVE CONDITIONAL CLAUSES IN LUTHER'S WRITINGS

But even if we were to concede that . . .

—Translation by Martin Bertram
of Luther, AE 22:137

This chapter will examine the controversial clause of LC II 66b in order to explain its grammatical structure and usage. It will draw on earlier points about the kinds of sentences Luther wrote for dialectical[1] and rhetorical purposes. Since an important feature of the debate about this clause has focused on whether the clause has indicative or subjunctive verbs and whether it is a statement of fact or a statement contrary to fact, these issues will be carefully considered here. However, another possibility will also be considered: the mood of the verbs may not be as important as the greater structure and content of the sentence and its context.

As noted in the introduction, Chapters 8 and 9 are the most difficult parts of this study. Please take your time reading them. Though I have tried to present things as simply and clearly as possible, I have also had to assume readers will understand essential, technical grammatical terms. If in doubt about the meaning of a technical term, please consult a standard collegiate dictionary.

CHALLENGING GRAMMAR

Concessive clauses are among the most difficult types of grammatical constructions. As one linguist noted,

> A certain support for the assumption that concessive constructions are especially complex semantically can be derived from the fact that they tend to develop in connection with the introduction of written forms of a language and are also acquired much later by children than other types of adverbial clauses.[2]

Luther used concessive clauses surprisingly often because of their dialectical and rhetorical qualities; they must be considered a major element of his style.

That Luther's concessive clauses have challenged translators before is demonstrated by the following example. While translating Luther's sermons on John,[3] Martin H. Bertram (1887–1983) encountered a clause that required special consideration. Bertram was familiar with issues of translation, having served for decades as a professor of German language and literature at Concordia College, St. Paul (1914–16); The Luther Institute (1916–21); Concordia Junior College, Fort Wayne (1921–57), and Concordia Senior College, Fort Wayne (1957–58). He was a prolific translator of numerous German books and documents,[4] including one of the most controversial texts in the American Edition of *Luther's Works*.[5] Bertram found that in commenting on John 1:17 Luther interrupted his main clause with a concessive clause[6] that was contrary to fact. One could translate this passage literally as follows:

> . . . whoever they [the saints] are, though I suppose that they were full of grace, they still could not impart the self-same things to me.[7]

Though such a translation can be understood, it makes awkward, confusing English. The passage begins with "whoever they are [*wer sie sind*]," but it is interrupted by Luther's thought, "though I suppose [*ich setze aber*]."[8] With the word "though [*aber*]" Luther denotes a *concession*. In other words, he *concedes* a point for the sake of argument. The conclusion of the passage, "still . . . not [*so . . . doch . . . nicht*]," emphasizes to the reader that the concession is hypothetical or contrary to fact. Ultimately, Luther has not conceded anything.

Because of this grammar, Bertram had to choose between an awkward English sentence—more "faithful" to the wording of the German—and a smoother English sentence that clearly presented Luther's meaning. Bertram decided on a freer translation:

> But even if we were to concede that they were full of grace, they would still be unable to impart any of it to me.[9]

Note that Bertram translated Luther's expression with an appropriate English expression, using "even if we were to *concede*" in order to make the *concessive* grammar obvious. Bertram's solution is not the only way to translate the passage. Nonetheless, it was an effective way to express clearly Luther's complex thought, which was rooted in rhetoric and dialectic.

AN OVERVIEW OF CONCESSIVE CONDITIONAL CLAUSES

Before considering the complex *ob . . . gleich*[10] concessive clause Luther used in LC II 66b, a broader description of concessive clauses may prove helpful. This is not intended as a comprehensive description of all concessive clauses (the varieties are remarkable) but as background for understanding LC II 66b. The focus will be on a particular type of concessive construction: concessive conditionals, [11] that is, concessions that propose a condition that is either factual or counterfactual.

Luther's use of concessive clauses is known to all Lutherans through a famous example: verse 3 of "A Mighty Fortress," where one reads:

> Though devils all the world should fill, . . . we tremble not.[12]

This passage can illustrate in English many of the concessive constructions Luther used in the Large Catechism and the Smalcald Articles.

The Form of Concessive
Conditional Constructions

Concessive constructions can be described by their form and their content. We shall describe form first. The form of a concessive construction depends on whether it appears before or after the main clause.[13] For example, consider the following:

 [conclusion]   [condition][14]
[EX 1] We are calm, though devils are in the world.
 [condition]   [conclusion]
[EX 2] Though devils are in the world, we are calm.

For Luther, the concession of EX 1 is usually added as further information. By contrast, the form of EX 2 is usually used for rhetorical and dialectical argument.[15] The conclusion is often introduced by "still" or "yet" (Ger. *so*).[16]

The Content of Concessive Conditional Clauses

Concessive clauses may appear with positive or negative conclusions. They may also be distinguished as statements of fact, statements contrary to fact, and rhetorically absurd or extreme statements.[17] Here are English examples of concessive clauses with positive conclusions (beginning with the two forms noted above):

EX 1	We are calm, though devils are in the world.	Statement of fact
EX 2	Though devils are in the world, we are calm.	
EX 3	We are calm, though devils may be in the world.	Statement contrary to fact
EX 4	Though devils may be in the world, we are calm.	
EX 5	We are calm, though devils should fill all the world.	Absurd or extreme statement
EX 6	Though devils all the world should fill, we are calm.	

Most commonly, concessive clauses use indicative or subjunctive mood verbs. An indicative mood verb indicates or declares something in a factual way. A subjunctive mood verb declares that something is possible (a proposition), doubtful, or desirable (a wish). The subordinate clause in EX 1 and 2, as a statement of fact, uses an indicative mood verb for the condition. EX 3 and 4 use a subjunctive mood verb in the condition. It describes something that is proposed as a possibility, not an established fact. The condition for EX 5 and 6 also uses a subjunctive mood verb. However, these latter examples add further conditions to the clause ("fill all"), taking the possibility to an absurd extreme. In this way, EX 5 and 6 have the greatest rhetorical effect. In other words, they present the sharpest argument with the greatest contrast between the condition and the conclusion.

A concessive clause may also have a negative conclusion, which is the form Luther used in verse 3 of "A Mighty Fortress."

EX 7	We tremble not, though devils are in the world.	Statement of fact
EX 8	Though devils are in the world, we tremble not.	
EX 9	We tremble not, though devils may be in the world.	Statement contrary to fact
EX 10	Though devils may be in the world, we tremble not.	
EX 11	We tremble not, though devils all the world should fill.	Absurd or extreme statement
EX 12	Though devils all the world should fill, we tremble not.	

As before, the subordinate clause in EX 7 and 8 is a statement of fact and uses an indicative mood verb. In EX 9 and 10, a statement contrary to fact uses a subjunctive mood verb in the condition. EX 11 and 12 use a subjunctive mood verb and all-inclusive terms ("fill all") in the condition to present an absurd extreme, which contrasts most sharply with the conclusion. In other words, the conclusion states a fact. The condition states a "logical possibility" taken to the extreme.[18]

MEASURES OF RHETORIC IN CONCESSIVE CONDITIONAL CLAUSES

Rhetoric often expresses itself in specific forms.[19] General observations can be made about the depth of rhetoric in the concessive clauses above. Consider the following general distinctions, which illustrate the progression of the rhetoric:

- Level 1 (informational): conclusion-condition format
- Level 2 (rhetorical): condition-conclusion format
- Level 3 (more rhetorical): condition-conclusion; negative conclusion
- Level 4 (most rhetorical): condition-conclusion; negative conclusion; all-inclusive/exclusive terms; or condition-conclusion; negation clause added; all-inclusive/exclusive terms

As more conditional features are added to the sentence, the level of rhetoric usually increases. Statements of fact appear most often at the informational level (this will be demonstrated later with examples from Luther). But when a sentence has more rhetorical features, these features increase the likelihood that the condition is contrary to fact, or even absurd. With these features a writer softens or sharpens his argument in order to achieve the desired persuasive effect with the reader.

CONCLUSION

Concessive clauses are very complex semantically. There is a wide variety of forms and qualifiers for these constructions. In view of the examples above, one may describe the concessive construction in LC II 66b ("although they believe in, and worship, only one true God") in the following ways: (1) it has a condition-conclusion format designed for dialectical and rhetorical purposes ("although . . . yet"), (2) it uses an exclusive term ("only"), and (3) it has a negative conclusion ("yet know not"), which contrasts sharply with the concessive clause. These features would typically move the reader toward a contrary to fact understanding of the clause.

NOTES

1. Linguist Violeta Ramsey observes, "The study of the different types of adverbial clauses in the past has been done almost exclusively by logicians, who analyzed the relationship between the adverbial clause and the main clause in terms of truth value, material implication, presupposition, etc." Violeta Ramsey, "The Functional Distribution of Preposed and Postposed 'If' and 'When' Clauses in Written Discourse," in *Coherence and Grounding in Discourse*, ed. Russell S. Tomlin (Philadelphia: John Benjamins Publishing Company, 1987), 383–408. Linguists are now studying these long-recognized dialectical constructions (whether formal or informal). Claudio Di Meola reviewed the writings of linguists on the relationship between concessivity as a grammatical category and as a dialectical/logical category. Some linguists have wanted to abandon the term "concessive" in order to make a separation of the grammar from dialectic, but Di Meola retained the traditional terminology. Claudio Di Meola, *Der Audsdruck der Konzessivatät in der deutschen Gegenwartssprache: Theorie und Beschreibung anhand eines Vergleichs mit dem Italienischen* (Tübingen: Max Niemeyer Verlag, 1997), 14–16. "Die Konzession impliziert demnach eine Art virtueller Argumentation: Der Sprecher weist auf ein mögliches . . . Das Argument wird als potentiell relevant anerkannt: es wird "konzediert," daß jemand aufgrund von *p* zu dem Schluß *q* kommen könnte" (15).

2. Ekkehard König, "Concessive Clauses," in *Encyclopedia of Language and Literature*, 2nd ed. (Oxford: Elsevier, 2006), II:821. In *Grammaticalization* (Cambridge: Cambridge University Press, 1993), Paul J. Hopper and Elizabeth Closs Traugott note, "Concessive meanings develop late in the history of specific clause linkage makers partly because the concessive is more abstract, partly because it is more complex logically" (180). Also, "Concessive connectives seem to have developed fairly late in the history of the languages for which we have evidence. There were few, if any clearly concessive markers in . . . Old High German." König, "Concessive Connectives and Concessive Sentences," 151.

3. AE 22.

4. Martin H. Bertram translated the following works: AE 13:1–38 (1956); "Sermons on the Gospel of St. John," AE 22–24 (1957–61); Heinrich Bornkamm, *Luther's World of Thought* (St. Louis: CPH, 1958); AE 30 (1967); AE 43:3–70, 81–112 (1968); Peter Brunner, *Worship in the Name of Jesus* (St. Louis: CPH, 1968); AE 42 (1969); AE 47 (1971); AE 15:265–351 (1972); Werner Elert, *The Lord's Supper Today* (St. Louis, CPH, 1973); AE 28:59–213 (1973); AE 19:35–106 (1974); Werner Elert, *The Christian Faith: An Outline of Lutheran Dogmatics* (Columbus, OH: Lutheran Theological Seminary, 1974). Bertram also wrote and compiled *Stimmen der Kirche* (St. Louis: CPH, 1961).

5. "On the Jews and Their Lies," AE 47:121–306 (Philadelphia: Muhlenberg Press, 1971).

6. "The term 'concessive' belongs to the terminological inventory that traditional grammar makes available for the characterization and classification of adverbials and adverbial clauses." König, "Concessive Clauses," II:820.

7. Translation by Edward Engelbrecht. The German is as follows: ". . . wer sie sind, ich setze aber, das sie voler gnade weren, so können sie mire doch dieselbige nicht mitteilen." WA 46:655, lines 32–33.

8. This is a subordinate clause governed by a subordinating conjunction (*aber*).

9. AE 22:137. The editor for this volume was J. Pelikan.

10. "'*Ob . . . gleich*,' the separated form of this conjunction, is obsolete in modern German. The conditional use of *ob* has been obsolete for a long time (*ob jemand sündiget, so haben wir einen Fürsprecher* [Luther]: 'if somebody sins, we have an advocate') and survives only in the construction *ob . . . oder* 'whether . . . or not' (*ob du willst oder nicht, du musst kommen* 'like it or not, you have to come')." Claudio di Meola, "Synchronic Variation as a Result of Grammaticalization: Concessive Subjunctives in German and Italian," *Linguistics* 39, no. 1 (2001), 132. See also *The Oxford-Duden German Dictionary*, rev. ed. (Oxford: Clarendon Press, 1997), 547. See *Wörterbuch der deutschen Gegenwartssprache*, vol. 4 (Berlin: Akademie-Verlag, 1974), 2681. *Muret-Sanders Encyclopädisches Wörterbuch der englischen und deutschen Sprache* (Berlin: Langenscheidtsche Verlagsbuchhandlung, 1905), II:1513. The entry for *ob* notes, "3. (mit konzessivsatz) ob . . . auch, ob . . . gleich, ob . . . schon (al)though, even if." See also Jacob Grimm and Wilhelm Grimm, *Deutsches Wörterbuch*, vol. 7 (Leipzig: S. Hirzel, 1889), 1054–55. They list *ob* combining with various other words to indicate a concessive clause, and they provide numerous examples from literature. *Der Grosse Duden: Grammatik*, vol. 4 (Mannheim/Zurich: Bibliographisches Institut, 1966), entry 3590e describes *ob* as a subordinating conjunction that forms the concessive. The separated *ob . . . gleich* form has not been in use for centuries. Some modern German dictionaries do not have an entry for the separated form. For example, the popular *Cassell's German-English, English-German Dictionary* (New York: MacMillan, 1978) does not list the separated form; it does include the combined form *obgleich*, which is typically translated "though" or "although" for modern German. "In many languages, concessive connectives are composed of a conditional (e.g., G[erman]. *wenn*, originally conditional (e.g. E[nglish]. *though*, G[erman]. *ob*) . . . and /or an additive or emphatic focus particle like E[nglish]. *also, even, too*." König, "Concessive Connectives and Concessive Sentences," 153.

11. "In addition to conditional and concessive sentences most languages have developed a sentence type (viz. 'concessive conditionals') that shares properties with both of the two former categories: . . . [example:] Even if I try very hard, I won't manage." König, "Concessive Connectives and Concessive Sentences," 147.

12. "Und wenn die Welt voll Teuffel wer' . . . So fürchten wir uns nicht so sehr, . . ." (WA 35:456).

13. Linguists refer to "preposed" and "postposed" clauses. See Ramsey, 383–408.

14. "Conclusion" and "condition" are used for the traditional terms *protasis* and *apodosis*.

15. Ramsey uses English literature to make the following observations, which correspond well with examples of concessive clauses from Luther. (Please note: the observations above about Luther's German were made prior to corroboration from Ramsey's research with English grammar.)

Preposed I[f] C[lauses] . . . are thematically associated to the preceding discourse as well as to the main clause, thus [they] have a broader scope. *Postposed* I[f] C[lauses] . . . are only related to their main clause, [they] thus have a very localized scope. . . . [based on examples] the initial clauses associate with a portion of the discourse that precedes them, the examples show how their scope goes many clauses back and how they help the dynamics of the sequencing of information. The final clauses, on the contrary, carry information that is not exactly part of the main line of the narrative, which makes them look more like a parenthetical comment for the main clause. . . . The initial clause is 'recalling' part of the preceding discourse and in so doing it is connecting or grounding that preceding discourse to the material that follows. In this way it calls for a pause before the introduction of the information conveyed by the main clause. On the other hand the postposed clause only seems to be extending the semantic information given by the main clause, thus its role is not at the thematic level. . . . the *positioning* of the adverbial clause, before or after the main clause, is determined by the organization of discourse. (385, 405–7)

More will be stated about this in the next chapter.

16. Luther often ended the construction with "so doch," as was typical in Middle High German and in the sixteenth century. Carl Franke, *Grundzüge der Schriftsprache Luthers*, 3 Vols. (Halle: Der Buchhandlung des Waisenhauses, 1922) III:368, § 198 4 d d. Linguists describe these as "strengthening elements." They may be added to the concessive conjunction or used elsewhere in the sentence. "Concessive sentences may also have developed by a process called 'strengthening.' . . . This term refers to the introduction of emphatic particles like E[nglish]. *all* (*be it +all>albeit*; *all+though>although*), G[erman]. *wohl, zwar, gleich, schon*." König, "Concessive Connectives and Concessive Sentences," 159. Di Meola surveyed a large body of modern German literature and collected 2,234 examples of all types of concessive constructions. In 145 examples (6.5 percent), the main clause had "strengthening elements": 92 examples had *doch*; 60 examples had *so*. In 32 examples, *so . . . doch* appeared together (approx. 1.5 percent). For *obgleich* constructions, *doch* appeared only twice; *so* appeared only once. For *wenngleich*, *doch* appeared only once. His *obgleich* and *wenngleich* examples had strengthening elements in only 3.84 percent of cases. Di Meola (1997), 200–207. By contrast, in the 59 examples listed from Luther (Appendix D), *obgleich* and *wenngleich* constructions have *so, doch,* or *so . . . doch* 24 times, that is, in 40.6% of cases! Luther used these strengthening elements ten times more frequently than the sampling from modern German writers. Though this could represent differences in the type of literature or a diachronic change in usage, it may represent a significant feature of Luther's rhetorical and dialectical style. Other sixteenth-century writers do not use these *obgleich* and *wenngleich* constructions as often (Di Meola, *Audsdruck der Konzessivatät*; also see Chapter 9, note 1), much less with so many strengthening elements.

17. "The situation described by a sentence with a concessive clause is an exception to a general tendency and therefore remarkable." König, "Concessive Clauses," 821.

J. Bennett demonstrates the difference between a condition and an extreme or absurd condition in "Even if," *Linguistics and Philosophy* 5 (1982): 413. The term *even* takes things to the extreme in a proposition. So, "if p, then q" is definitely different from "Even if p, then still q." Peter Matheson notes how Luther enjoyed taking arguments "to absurd lengths." *The Rhetoric of the Reformation*, (Edinburgh: T & T Clark, 1998), 123.

18. Franke, III:325, § 2 C ß. He cites Isaiah 49:15 from the Luther Bible as an example: "And even if [*ob*] they themselves should forget, yet [*so . . . doch*] I will not [*nicht*] forget you." Translation by Edward Engelbrecht.

19. See Chapters 6 and 7 on dialectic and rhetoric.

Chapter 9

VERB MOODS AND MEANING IN LUTHER'S WRITINGS

One should keep to grammar the hours before noon, so that the pupils may be well drilled in this. . . . When they have sufficiently studied grammar they may use these hours for dialectic and rhetoric.

—Martin Luther, AE 40:319

This chapter will make observations about Luther's choice of verb moods based on the example sentences listed in Appendix D.

INDICATIVE AND SUBJUNCTIVE

Concessions with *ob . . . gleich, obgleich, wenn . . . gleich,* and *wenngleich*[1] typically use indicative or subjunctive mood verbs, though other verbs are possible (see Appendix D chart: CC11 and CC38, passive infinitives; CC21, modal verb).[2] The indicative mood is usually used for statements of fact.[3] The subjunctive mood is usually used for statements contrary to fact (logical possibility and extreme or absurd statements).[4] A number of verbal forms can be either indicative or subjunctive because they have the same spelling in both moods. A reader must interpret them based on the context.[5] This is exactly the issue in LC II 66b, where the verbs *glauben* and *anbeten* can be either present active indicative, third person plural, or present active subjunctive, third person plural.[6]

Another complication is that Luther is not always consistent in his spelling of verb forms. Also, contracted forms were used in the sixteenth century (e.g., for CC13 the *Triglotta* has "*wärest,*" a subjunctive ending; the Die Bekenntnisschriften der evangelisch-lutherischen Kirche (BKS) has "*wärst,*" which appears indicative, since the "e" has dropped out).[7] These factors do not make the mood of the verbs impossible to determine, since context adds clarity. However, by comparing and contrasting the structures of the clauses, one can also reach helpful conclusions about whether a verb is indicative or subjunctive. The tabulations below are based on the fifty-nine examples in the chart in Appendix D. The sampling was based on the *Triglotta* text.

First, a general comparison:

All Examples	
Indicative	19
Indicative or Subjunctive	16
Subjunctive	19
Other	5

The samples show a balanced spread between the indicative and subjunctive moods. But analysis of specific structures yields different results. For example, the conclusion-condition sentences break down as follows:

Conclusion-Condition	
Indicative	13
Indicative or Subjunctive	7
Subjunctive	7
Other	3

The conclusion-condition format favors the indicative mood. This is to be expected since this format in most cases simply adds further information. Next, consider the condition-conclusion format:

Condition-Conclusion	
Indicative	7
Indicative or Subjunctive	8
Subjunctive	12
Other	2

OTHER QUALIFYING FEATURES

As one might expect, condition-conclusion sentences, which Luther prefers for rhetorical and dialectical effect, favor the subjunctive mood. Further qualifications show even greater variance.

Concessions with All-inclusive or Exclusive Terms	
Indicative	3
Indicative or Subjunctive	4
Subjunctive	11
Other	2

Concessive Constructions with Negations	
Indicative	2
Indicative or Subjunctive	5
Subjunctive	8

Based on format and content, thirteen key examples most fully parallel the sentence in LC II 66b (examples in bold on the chart, Appendix D). Here is a tabulation of their moods:

Key Examples (LC II 66 Included)	
Indicative	2
Indicative or Subjunctive	5
Subjunctive	7

CONCLUSION

Other examples of Luther's concessive constructions closely parallel the structure of LC II 66b. These constructions favor the subjunctive mood, which forms contrary-to-fact statements. Given the features and structure of LC II 66b, the verbs of the concessive clause are likely subjunctive. The statement is likely contrary to fact.

NOTES

1. Each of these forms will be considered because of the similar ways they are used. Luther uses these concessive conjunctions in much the same way. See Franke,

III:367–68, §198d. Franke lists them as parallel constructions. The number of concessive conjunctions used in Luther's time was vast and included the following: *ob, ob ja, ob joch, ob auch, obgleich, obschon, obwol, obzwar, wenn auch, wenn gleich, wenn schon, wiewol,* and *so schon.* Listed from Joseph Kehrein, *Grammatik der deutschen Sprache des funfzehnten bis siebenzehnten Jahrhunderts* (Hildsheim: Georg Olms, 1968), III:268, §498. Examples of *wenn . . . gleich* appear more often than *ob . . . gleich* in the grammars. This is probably because Luther does not use *ob . . . gleich* very often in his translation of the Bible, which the grammars frequently cite for examples of Luther's constructions. (*Ob . . . gleich* is the most common concessive construction in the Large Catechism.) Luther's work on translating the Bible was guided by a commission including John Bugenhagen, Justas Jonas, Caspar Creutziger, Phillip Melanchthon, Matthew Aurogallum, Georg Rörer, and others. See M. Reu, *Luther's German Bible* (Columbus, OH: The Lutheran Book Concern, 1934), 212, 234. It may be that the influence of the commission edited out Luther's tendency to use *ob . . . gleich.* A cursory search of German hymns for *ob . . . gleich* and *obgleich* revealed that some other writers from the sixteenth century use these terms as Luther did. The terms also show up in a number of Paul Gerhardt's hymns. After Gerhardt (1607–76), they virtually disappear from German hymns.

2. The subjunctive mood later gave way to modal constructions. Franke, III:309–10, §177.

3. Franke, *Grundzüge,* Vol. III, §178–82.

4. Ibid., §183–87.

5. In other words, morphology alone cannot be definitive.

6. Students of German may see these forms side by side in Henry Sturtz, *501 German Verbs* (New York: Barron's, 1982), 45, 156. In *Die Bekenntnisschriften der evangelisch-lutherischen Kirche*, the umlaut on verbal forms of *glauben* probably represents a dialectical vocalization of the verb. It appears in some editions of the *Book of Concord* but not others. The umlaut is represented in the original 1580 edition of the *Book of Concord* by the spelling "*gleuben*," with the "e" standing in for "ä." The same spelling can be seen in the text of the Large Catechism in *Luthers Werke* Vol. 30, pt. I (Weimar: Hermann Bohlaus, 1910). The Johann Andreas Detzer edition (Nürnberg, 1847), the Berlin edition (1851), the *Concordien-Buch* (New York, 1859), and *Concordia Triglotta* (St. Louis, 1921) lack this umlaut for *glauben.* See Franke, I:127, §44; Kehrein, I:50, §74.

7. Franke provides extensive examples of such changes in II:291–366, §§134–66. Such contracted forms are still used today.

Chapter 10
SUMMARY ANALYSIS OF LC II 66

The Gospel wants to be taught and preached always and always, in order that it may always appear above the horizon.[1]

—Martin Luther on the mission of the Church

This chapter will draw on the dialectical, rhetorical, and grammatical portions of the study to provide a summary analysis.

In an article on LC II 66b, John Nordling concluded that the Latin text[2] could not support a statement-of-fact interpretation of the clause. His article added the following comment about the German text:

> This borders on what grammarians call a contrary to fact statement: "Even if it were the case [understand: but it is not!] that they believe in, and worship, only one true God. . .," etc.[3]

Nordling's article interpreted the passage as contrary to fact, though it did not argue that Luther's German grammar, rhetoric, and dialectic insist on such an understanding. Also, the bracketed wording in Nordling's article—"[understand: but it is not!]"—presented the clause as a *per impossibile* argument. This chapter will argue that the proposal in Nordling's article was, in fact, correct.

As presented earlier, Luther's argument about "all outside Christianity" actually began in LC II 63b when he wrote:

> For although the whole world with all diligence has endeavored to ascertain what God is, what He has in mind and does, yet has she never been able to attain to [Latin: the knowledge and understanding of] any of these things. But here [in the Creed] we have everything in richest measure.

This presents Luther's consistent theological opinion that no one by his own reason or strength can truly know and believe in the one true God. The first and last sentences of paragraph LC II 66b show that the passage is not about finding common points of belief between various religions and Christianity. Instead, the paragraph emphasizes the division and separation of Christians from "all other people on earth."[4] Luther makes "all other people on earth" the subject of the verbs in the second and third sentences:

> All outside of Christianity, whether heathen, Turks, Jews, or false Christians and hypocrites . . . they . . . they . . . they . . .[5]

Note well how Luther begins LC II 66b with an exclusive expression, "all outside." Next, he interrupts his thought to list "all outside of Christianity." The list heaps together one group after another. He starts with the most obvious unbelievers, "heathen," yet goes on to reach into the congregation of professing Christians! Then Luther adds his concession with the *ob . . . gleich* construction. All these features build on one another like a series of steps. By the time Luther reaches the concession, he has reached the height of rhetorical and dialectical force.[6] The negation in the conclusion ("yet [they] know not") leaps from the high point of the argument back to sober reality. Because these groups do not have Christ, they cannot know the one true God's mind or His blessings. They do not truly believe in and worship the one true God.

For the concession, Luther used one of his most complex constructions, with multiple features: condition-conclusion format, *ob . . . gleich*, the exclusive term "only," and a *so . . . doch nicht* negation in the conclusion. The use of "only" in the clause is especially important. As noted above in Chapter 7, Luther placed special emphasis on such all-inclusive and exclusive terms because of his training in medieval rhetoric and dialectic. It cannot be stated factually that "all outside of Christianity" have *only* one true God. Luther clearly understood that the heathen—as a group—had multiple gods. The exclusive "all outside," the breadth of the list, and the use of "only" in the concession drive a reader to conclude that Luther's concession is contrary to fact. Because the concession is contrary to fact, the verbs in the concession are most likely subjunctive.[7]

However, one may also recall Luther's explanation of Paul's *per impossibile* argument in 1 Corinthians 15 (Chapter 6). His argument does not necessarily have to use the subjunctive mood. Paul used indicative mood verbs, and Luther translated them with indicative mood verbs. This demonstrates that even though the general trend is for Luther to use subjunctive mood verbs for such arguments, he does not have to use them necessarily. In the end, whether the verbs of the concessive clause in LC II 66b are indicative or subjunctive, the broader context and *per impossibile* structure of the argument are most significant for interpreting the meaning of the clause.

A COMMENT ON THE LATIN TRANSLATION

The Latin translation of the Large Catechism (1529) was provided by Vincent Obsopoeus, rector of the school at Ansbach.[8] In most cases, Obsopoeus translated *ob . . . gleich* concessive clauses with subjunctive mood verbs in Latin—even in cases where the German is clearly indicative (see Appendix D). This may be because Latin naturally prefers the subjunctive for such constructions, as also happens with French.[9] Concessive clauses beginning with *quamquam* use the subjunctive commonly in imperial, medieval, and humanist Latin.

Nordling and Kopff identified an ACI construction (accusative with infinitive) in LC II 66. An ACI construction is used to present indirect speech, that is, a statement of a claim. The grammar of Obsopoeus's translation differs in character from the German grammar. His translation is idiomatic rather than literal.

It should be noted that in German grammar contrary-to-fact statements are associated with statements of indirect speech (see

Franke III.183). Likewise, the conjunction *ob. . .gleich* is used for indirect speech.[10] To understand Obsopoeus's reasoning, grammarians may wish to examine these relationships more closely.

It seems that Obsopoeus also used an ACI construction to translate another *ob . . . gleich* concessive clause earlier in the catechism (LC, Preface 9; *Triglotta*, 568). Study of Obsopoeus's translation may prove helpful for understanding his translation at LC II 66.

CONCLUSION

Luther's grammar, rhetoric, and dialectic all point to a contrary to fact interpretation of the concessive conditional clause in LC II 66. This is true whether the verbs are in the indicative mood or the subjunctive mood. The passage emphasizes the uniqueness of the Church, to which the Lord has entrusted the Gospel for the salvation of all people.

NOTES

1. Cited from Werner Elert, "The Church," in *The Structure of Lutheranism*, trans. Walter A. Hansen (St. Louis: CPH, 1962), 387. See WA 10 I, 540.
2. For more on the Latin text and its relationship to the German, see the end of this chapter.
3. Nordling, 239n17.
4. Luther here returns to a theme introduced earlier at LC II 56, "But outside of this Christian Church, where the Gospel is not, there is no forgiveness, as also there can be no holiness [sanctification]."
5. The singular pronoun "*es*" in LC II 66b reaches back to the singular pronoun "*was*." This pronoun reaches back to the collective noun "*Leuten*" in LC II 66a. Some interpreters may seek to separate "heathen, Turks, Jews" from "false Christians and hypocrites" in order to make the latter groups the subject of the controversial clause. However, this interpretation does not fit the grammar and larger context of the passage. With "*oder*" Luther did make a distinction between people who do not profess to be Christians (heathen, Turks, Jews) and those who do profess to be Christians (false Christians and hypocrites). However, all five groups listed as "all outside Christianity" remain the subjects of the verbs. See Kopff.
6. Nordling, examining the Latin, concludes that the clause is "highly rhetorical" (239).
7. It is noteworthy that *Unser Glaube: Die Bekenntnisschriften der evangelisch-lutherische Kirche*, 3rd ed., ed. Horst Georg Pöhlmann (Gütersloher: Gütersloher Verlagshaus Gerd Mohn, 1991) has updated the language of LC II 66 by using the

auxiliary verb *mögen* (695). The result is similar to Lenker's translation of the LC, who noted the verb was subjunctive (see quote, p. 121). A more direct modern German wording is "auch wenn sie nur einen wahrhaftigen Gott glauben und anbeten," in R. Mau, *Evangelische Bekenntnisse: Bekenntnisschriften der Reformation und neuere Theologische Erklärungen*, vol. 2 (Bielefeld: Luther-Verlag, 1997), 95. The words *auch wenn* translate as "even if." See Hubert Jannach, *German for Reading Knowledge*, 3rd ed. (Boston: Heinle & Heinle Publications, Inc., 1980), 176–77. Jannach provides examples of contrary-to-fact constructions using *wenn*, which is typical in modern German. See also Walter F. W. Lohnes and F. W. Strothmann, *German: A Structural Approach*, 3rd ed. (New York: W. W. Norton & Company, 1980), 257. Another issue raised for this passage is the use of the definite article ("the") before "one true God," provided first by Theodore Tappert and subsequently provided by F. Samuel Janzow and Robert Kolb and Timothy Wengert. See Manteufel, 366–69. One may note that although the definite article does not appear in the German, the words "one, true" have likely compelled the translators to supply the definite article.

8. See Bente, 195.

9. "Concessive connectives co-occur with the subjunctive mood in many languages (e.g. French)." König, "Concessive Connectives," 154.

10. See Daniel Sanders, *Wörterbuch der Hauptschwierigkeiten in der deutschen Sprache* (Berlin: Langenscheidtsche Verlags-Buchhandlung, 1894), 180, 220.

Chapter 11

TRANSLATING LC II 66

Where literal accuracy and clarity have conflicted, it is clarity that we have preferred, so that sometimes paraphrase seemed more faithful than literal fidelity.[1]

—Jaroslav Pelikan, Preface to the
American Edition of *Luther's Works*

This chapter will present various options for translating LC II 66b in view of its broader context and in view of the readers of the translation.

A LITERAL TRANSLATION

Based on Luther's dialectic, rhetoric, grammar, and theology, the best literal translation of the concessive clause in LC II 66b was provided by the Henkel edition:

Even if[2] they believe in and worship only one true God . . .

The modern German edition by Mau likewise provides this type of literal wording. The translations using "though" and "although" are not sufficiently clear, since they are easily misinterpreted as statements of fact. However, the Henkel translation can also be misunderstood since "even if" can be used to introduce a statement of fact in English (e.g., "He is my friend, even if he *is* a fool.").

TRANSLATIONS WITH AUXILIARY VERBS

A second category of translations was introduced by Lenker. This category supplies an auxiliary verb to signal that the verbs of the clause are subjunctive. The difficulty with this approach is that the wording leaves too much in the realm of possibility. Also, the auxiliary verb can imply misleading things about the text.

- Even if they may believe in and worship only one true God . . .
- Even if they would believe in and worship only one true God . . .
- Even if they might believe in and worship only one true God . . .
- Even if they should believe in and worship only one true God . . .

The first three examples imply that Luther is in doubt about whether "all those outside of Christianity" truly believe in and worship the one true God. The sentence with "should" implies that the groups can know Him apart from Christ or may have a duty to believe.

Two other examples with auxiliary verbs are stronger:

- Even if they did believe in and worship only one true God . . .
- Even if they were to believe in and worship only one true God . . .

However, these also could be misread. The first example here could imply that these groups did believe in the past. The second could imply that God intends for them to believe in and worship Him apart from Christ, but something is preventing them. Such misreadings would violate the theological context of the passage.

IDIOMATIC TRANSLATIONS

These issues of clarity and potential misunderstanding led the editors of *Concordia: The Lutheran Confessions* to provide an idiomatic translation,[3] not unlike that provided in the Nordling article. A third option is also included:

- Even if we were to concede that . . . [they] believe in and worship only one true God . . . [Concordia][4]
- Even if it were the case [understand: but it is not!] that they believe in, and worship, true God . . . [Nordling]
- Even if they were [now] believing in and worshiping only one true God . . .

Although the idiomatic translations are more wordy, they are not subject to the misunderstandings described above. They clearly convey Luther's rhetoric, dialectic, and theology, though they do not convey them literally. Another possible idiomatic wording would make the *per impossibile* argument explicit as follows:

- Even if they believe in and worship only one true God [which is impossible] . . .

Such wording may be the best solution since it represents Luther's German literally yet also clearly shows the force of Luther's argument and counterfactual concession.

As demonstrated above, experienced translators such as Bertram at times chose freer, idiomatic translations in order to make the meaning of the text most clear for their readers.[5] The challenges presented by LC II 66b and the controversy surrounding the passage demonstrate why translation remains an art and will always remain a matter of discussion and even conflict.

CONCLUSION

There are numerous ways to translate the passage. A literal translation does not clearly represent the contrary-to-fact character of the clause. Translations using auxiliary verbs can be misleading. Idiomatic translations can make the meaning clearer. Representing the clause as a *per impossibile* argument may be the best option.

NOTES

1. See note 5 for more on Pelikan's statement.
2. "Note also that E[nglish] *even* has changed its meaning from an element basically asserting identity . . . into an expression characterizing its focus value as an

extreme, highly unlikely value for a given propositional schema." König, "Concessive Connectives and Concessive Sentences," 161. In other words, *even* expresses the extreme and surprising nature of the condition. "The whole force of the word 'even' is to introduce those extra implications." Bennett, 413. So, "if p, then q" is definitely different from "even if p, then still q."

3. Such translations are described as "paraphrases" by some scholars. This designation can be misleading since paraphrases are generally produced without reference to the original language and grammar of a text. For the translations above, the original languages of the texts and their grammar were carefully considered.

4. The translation resembles that provided by Bertram for AE 22:137. In the case of *Concordia: The Lutheran Confessions*, people who did not read German or Latin were actually sought out and invited to consider various potential translations of LC II 66. The editors noted how easily English readers might misunderstand various translations of the passage and therefore opted for an idiomatic translation. In this respect the editors were following Luther's counsel: "We do not have to inquire of the literal Latin, how we are to speak German. . . . Rather we must inquire about this of the mother in the home, the children on the street, the common man in the marketplace. We must be guided by their language, the way they speak, and do our translating accordingly." "On Translating: An Open Letter," in AE 35:189. Another helpful example can be seen at Ps 130:6. Luther translated the passage freely, "Meine Seele wartet auf den Herrn von einer Morgenwache bis zur andern," "My soul waits on the Lord from one morning-watch to the other." He adds "watch" and uses the expression "from one . . . to the other," omitting the repetition found in the original Hebrew. Luther did not argue that all translations of every passage must be free and idiomatic but that unclear literal passages should be translated more freely.

5. Regarding the Luther Bible, Reu explains, "The translation did not dare to be too literal, for both the Hebrew and the Greek languages have their own peculiarities, as well as the German, and the translation was to fit the genius of the German language, like the coat to the body. . . . his work was only half done when the verbal meaning of the original was understood; that was only the prelude to the equally difficult and sometimes even more difficult work of finding genuinely German equivalents." Reu, 261. See also AE 35:213–14. Jaroslav Pelikan, the general editor for the American Edition of *Luther's Works*, wrote, "We have tried throughout to translate Luther as he thought translating should be done. That is, we have striven for faithfulness on the basis of the best lexicographical materials available. But where literal accuracy and clarity have conflicted, it is clarity that we have preferred, so that sometimes paraphrase seemed more faithful than literal fidelity" (from the General Editors' Preface, which appears in each volume). By "paraphrase" Pelikan may mean translating phrase by phrase (rather than word by word), seeking expressions that convey the ideas best in English.

Chapter 12

Counter Arguments

O Lord our God, bestow on us Your rest and peace all the days of this life, that all the inhabitants of the earth may know You, that You are the only true God the Father, and You did send our Lord Jesus Christ, Your Son and Your beloved.

—Liturgy of Addai and Mari

A consideration of the evidence and the proposal of a conclusion would be incomplete without presenting arguments in support of a statement-of-fact interpretation of LC II 66b. Consider the following arguments.

The Authority Argument

Some will likely argue that, despite the data and analysis presented above, a majority of scholars support a statement-of-fact interpretation of the concessive conditional clause in LC II 66b. Since so few papers have been published on the text itself, the authority argument likely would be based on the various translations of LC II 66b. For example, someone might argue that the majority of translators favored a statement-of-fact translation rather than a contrary-to-fact translation.

Such an argument would not hold up to scrutiny for the following reasons: (1) three English translations clearly interpret the verbs of the concessive conditional clause in LC II 66b as subjunctive, which leads one to a contrary-to-fact interpretation (see Appendix E); (2) the remaining six English translations do not necessarily support a statement-of-fact interpretation since they are more or less ambiguous (they could represent a statement of fact or a statement contrary-to-fact interpretation); (3) one modern German edition clearly interprets the verbs as subjunctive and another is ambiguous (see note 7 in Chapter 10). For these reasons, the authority argument does not bear up against a contrary-to-fact interpretation of the clause. At best the authority argument could assert that a number of interpreters are not absolutely sure about the meaning of the passage.

THE EXCEPTION ARGUMENT

Some could argue that, in view of the data, the concessive conditional clause in LC II 66b represents an exception to the trends of the evidence. They could say that although Luther typically used such clauses to present contrary-to-fact statements, and although Luther persistently regarded the deities of other religions as idols or even demons, and although Luther had rejected the opinion that a person could approach God and know Him apart from Christ, he speaks in a different vein in LC II 66b.

However, this argument also has significant weaknesses. For example, (1) as exceptions, such passages can never prove the case. They cannot marshal sufficient evidence to overturn the general trends. They can only cast doubt. (2) The exception argument cannot call on evidence in all categories. There is no evidence that Luther believed people could genuinely come to know the one true God apart from Christ. Also, there is no evidence Luther believed that people of all religions actually worship the same, one true God.

THE SUBJECTIVE ARGUMENT

This would argue that Luther momentarily suspended his earlier conclusions and study of this topic and followed the opinion or desire of his heart, hoping that everyone would actually share his view of God. In view of the evidence compiled here, this argument is at best wishful thinking on the part of those who desire a kinder, gentler Luther.

Conclusion

Arguments in favor of a statement-of-fact interpretation of the concessive conditional clause in LC II 66b are difficult to defend. No doubt, some readers will wish to critique the conclusions of this document. Substantive critiques, based on research in the primary sources, will best serve this purpose. For example, a research paper that evaluates fifty-nine more examples from Luther's writings ca. 1529 would be most helpful. Critiques that seek only to raise doubt without providing clarity or answers or that indulge in speculations about personal or political motives will not serve the peace of the church nor aid in understanding these issues.

Chapter 13

CONCLUSION

We pray Thee, O Heavenly Father, that Thou wouldst again give Thy Holy Spirit to another, that he may gather Thy church anew everywhere together, that we may again live united and in Christian manner, and so by our good works, all unbelievers as Turks, Heathen, and Calicuts, may of themselves turn to us and embrace the Christian faith.[1]

—Albrecht Dürer, when he believed
Luther suffered martyrdom

A statement-of-fact interpretation of the concessive conditional clause in LC II 66 raises numerous theological and historical problems. It implies that Luther adopted doctrines like those of Erasmus or Zwingli on original sin, human reason and ability, faith, the work of the Spirit, salvation without knowledge of Christ, and knowledge of God. Those who prefer a statement-of-fact interpretation of the clause have likely not considered the legion of doctrinal and practical problems that result from their conclusion. Here again is a list of doctrines potentially affected by the interpretation of the passage:

- The nature of the Church (Ecclesiology)
- Natural knowledge of God (General Revelation)
- Revealed knowledge of God (Special Revelation)

- The power of human will and reason (Anthropology)
- The effects of original sin (Hamartiology)
- Grace (Soteriology)
- Faith and justification (Soteriology)
- Worship (Sanctification)
- Eternal punishment (Eschatology)

One might ask the following questions: If original sin does not prevent a person from believing in and worshipping the one true God, what need is there for the Holy Spirit? How serious is the human condition caused by original sin? If I can, by my own reason and strength, believe in and worship the one true God, do I really need Christ? If the one true God is rightly known, believed in, and worshipped through natural revelation, what need is there for the Holy Scripture? For the Church?

In contrast, interpreting the concessive conditional clause as a contrary-to-fact statement agrees with Luther's theology, history, dialectic, rhetoric, and grammar. Such an interpretation fits readily with what Luther persistently taught and with the clearer passages of doctrine in the Large Catechism. Common sense leads to a contrary-to-fact interpretation of the clause.

The Strengths of Our Church

The Lord has blessed Confessional Lutheranism with two historic strengths: (1) commitment to sound doctrine and (2) commitment to mission work. If Large Catechism II 66 is made to mean that Christians believe in and worship the same god proclaimed by other religions (the logical outcome of a statement-of-fact interpretation), that would undermine both sound doctrine and the urgent need to spread the Gospel.[2] In the text immediately before and after the controversial clause in LC II 66, Luther wrote,

> For although the whole world with all diligence has endeavored to ascertain what God is, what He has in mind and does, yet has she never been able to attain to [the knowledge and understanding of] any of these things. . . . These articles of the Creed, therefore, divide and separate

us Christians from all other people upon earth. . . . They [non-Christians] abide in eternal wrath and damnation. For they have not the Lord Christ, and, besides, are not illumined and favored by any gifts of the Holy Ghost. (LC II 63b, 66; *Triglotta*, 695–97)

Regrettably, since heathens, Turks, Jews, false Christians, and hypocrites do not know the triune God described in the three articles of the Creed, they "abide in eternal wrath" (see LC II 63–65).

The truths of this passage should spur all genuine Christians to fervent prayer, bold witness, and support for faithful mission work. Since the one true God—purely by grace—has called us by the Gospel of His Son through the work of the Holy Spirit, we have wonderful news to share with all people. Through Christ Jesus alone, all may know the one true God and receive salvation, for Christ gave His life for the sins of all people.

EPILOGUE

The truth of the Church is important. The peace of the Church is likewise important. It is our hope that the study of this document will promote both truth and peace so that God may bless and unite our service.

NOTES

1. Jane Campbell Hutchinson, *Albrecht Dürer: A Biography* (Princeton: Princeton University Press, 1990), 164–65. Dürer seems to have Matt 5:16 in mind for his prayer.
2. Consider also John 5:23b; 1 John 2:23; and 2 John 9.

Part 2

A Letter to the Commission on Doctrinal Review

Editor's Note

The following letter (July 8, 2005) is included for historical purposes and also because it was a resource for Chapter 5 of this study document. In the letter, CPH Publisher, Rev. Paul T. McCain provides a concise dogmatic treatment of issues related to LC II 66, citing Luther, the Confessions, and Holy Scripture. Changes have been made to the format of the letter but not to the content.

LUTHER, THE LUTHERAN CONFESSIONS, THE HOLY SCRIPTURES, AND LC II 66

We respectfully offer this paper to support the translation in *Concordia: The Lutheran Confessions* of LC II 66.

Even if we were to concede that everyone outside Christianity—whether heathen, Turks, Jews, or false Christians and hypocrites—believe in and worship only one true God, it would still be true that they do not know what His mind toward them is and cannot expect any love or blessing from Him.

The issue is what, if anything, in this sentence is contrary to God's Word and the Lutheran Confessions? As demonstrated in our other paper, "Understanding LC II 66," we believe the grammatical nuances in the original German clearly indicate that Luther is conceding what he knows is actually not true in order to make his main point. For the sake of clarity, we felt it important to offer the translation as we did in order to reflect as clearly for the English-speaking reader as possible the grammatical nuances.

LUTHER ON MUSLIMS, HEATHEN, UNBELIEVERS, AND BELIEF IN THE ONE TRUE GOD

What do we find elsewhere in Luther's writings that would shed light on his intention here in LC II 66? We surveyed nearly two thousand passages in Luther's writings where he comments about Muslims, worship, belief, faith, Christianity, and God. We could find not a single example where Luther asserts, without condition or qualification, that Muslims and other unbelievers actually do in fact worship and believe in the one true God.

Consistently throughout his writings Dr. Luther rejects Allah as a false god and refers to the Islamic religion as an instrument and work of Satan. Some claim that we are to look to Paul's speech at the Areopagus (Acts 17:22–31) as evidence that Muslims worship the true God. This is an incorrect assumption. Muslims *never* claim to worship an unknown god. There is nothing "unknown" about the god they worship. They worship Allah, about whom they say there is no god but Allah. But Allah is not the one *true* God. Allah is not the God and Father of our Lord Jesus Christ. As we will show, Luther believed that Allah is an idol, in fact the devil himself. The Holy Scripture and our Lutheran Confessions clearly distinguish between a general revelation to all mankind through creation and what is true actual "belief" and "worship" of the *true* God. The very fact that the Athenians describe an "unknown" god shows that unbelievers do not even know who the one true God is. If they do not, it is impossible to say that they actually do believe in and worship the one true God. The Augsburg Confession (AC) makes this point clear when it says flatly that the heathen are "without God" precisely because they do not have faith. Consider AC XX 24–25 and note carefully that it specifically rejects any suggestion that the heathen, that is unbelievers, have saving faith and worship the one true God.

Consider Luther's comment on the First Commandment in the Large Catechism, where he indicates that only "true faith" is what apprehends the one true God. Luther says,

> I have often said that the confidence and faith [*Glaube*] of the heart alone make both God and an idol. If your faith [*Glaube*] and trust is right, then your god is also true. On the other hand, if your trust is false and wrong, then you do not have the true God. For these two belong together, faith [*Glaube*] and God. (LC I 3)

In light of this comment, clearly Luther is not seriously suggesting, or stating as fact, in LC II 66 that unbelievers believe in and worship the one true God.

Permit us now to share a selection of quotations from *Luther's Works* that demonstrate what he thought so that we can better understand his remark in LC II. Many more quotations could be provided, but these are a good representative sampling.

Luther:

> Nature provides that we should call upon God. The Gentiles attest to this fact. For there never was a Gentile who did not call upon his idols, even though these were not the true God. (AE 35:168)

Again, Luther:

> Therefore it does not help our clergy [Roman Catholic] at all to allege that in their churches and chapters they serve no idol, but only God, the true Lord. For here you learn that *it is not enough to say or think, "I am doing it to God's glory; I have in mind the true God; I mean to be worshiping and serving the only God." All idolaters say and intend the very same thing. The thinking and intending is not what counts*, otherwise those who martyred the apostles and the Christians would also have been God's servants. For they too thought that they were offering a service to God, as Christ says in John 16[:2]; and St. Paul in Romans 10[:2] bears witness to the Jews that they have a zeal for God, and adds in Acts 26[:7] that with their worship night and day they hope to attain to the promised salvation. On the contrary let everyone see to it that he is certain his worship and service of God has been instituted by God's word, and not invented by his own pious notions or good intentions. *Whoever engages in a form of worship to which God has not borne witness ought to know that he is serving not the true God but an idol that he has concocted for himself.* (AE 35:272–73)

Again, Luther:

> *This all the Turks, Jews, monks, and hypocrites try to do*; for they all appear before God in the belief that He will regard their own or other persons' merits and sanctity, and will praise and extol them on this account. Such was the prayer of the hypocrite of whom we read in Luke 18:11: "God, I thank Thee that I am not like other men. (AE 24:88–89)

Again, Luther:

> What is more, when the Turks go into battle their only war cry is "Allah! Allah!" and they shout it till heaven and earth resound. But in the Arabic language Allah means God, and is a corruption of the Hebrew *Eloha.* For they have been taught in the Koran that they shall boast constantly with these words, "There is no God but God." *All that is really a device of the devil. For what does it mean to say, "There is no God but God," without distinguishing one God from another? The devil, too, is a god, and they honor him with this word; there is no doubt of that.* Therefore I believe that the Turks' Allah does more in war than they themselves. He gives them courage and wiles; he guides sword and fist, horse and man. What do you think, then, of the holy people who can call upon God in battle, and yet destroy Christ and all God's words and works, as you have heard? (AE 46:183)

Note: Luther specifically names "Allah" as no god at all, but the very devil himself.

Again, Luther:

> *All people who say that they mean the true God who created heaven and earth are lying.* They do not accept His work and Word but place their own thoughts above God and His Word. If they truly believed in a God who created heaven and earth, they would also know that as Creator this same God is also above their thoughts and possesses

the same authority to make, break and do as He pleases. But since they do not let Him be the Creator above them and their thoughts in so small a matter, *it cannot be true that they believe [Glaube] Him to be the Creator of all creation.* (Walch 10.I.1:241)

Again, Luther:

> It does Jews, Turks, and heretics no good to profess a very great devoutness and to boast against us Christians that they believe in the one God, the Creator of heaven and earth, and also call him "Father" with intense earnestness. For all that, their worship consists of nothing except futile and useless words that they use to take the name of God in vain and misuse it, against the Second Commandment. . . . Here you see that when they do not know who God is; and when they call Him "Creator" and "God" and "Father," they don't know what they are actually saying. . . . Therefore they have no God, but they misuse the name of "God" in sin and shame and invent their own god and creator, who is supposed to be their father and whose children they profess to be. (St. L 3:1932)

Again Luther:

> Jews, Turks, and Tartars all esteem Christ and His mother Mary very highly. But they do not believe [*glaube*] that He is the Son of God, in whom one must believe and through whom all are saved. . . . Therefore, *the faith of the Jews and the Turks is nothing but sheer blindness, for they exclude the Son and want to retain only the Father. This is the chief article of our Christian faith: that the Son is eternal and true God, and also true man, sent into the world for its salvation. This article annuls the belief [glaube] of the Jews, the Turks, and all others who renounce the Son and thus worship another god and look to another source for help. The Turk is not able to pray the Lord's Prayer or the articles of the Creed. Faith, to which God alone is entitled, is the chief type*

of worship. For we are not to believe in angels, prophets, or apostles. No, this divine honor is due the Son alone; for He is true God with the Father. John treats this article very intensively. . . . If I earnestly believe that Christ is true God and that He became our Savior, I will never deny this but will proclaim it publicly against the Turks, the world, the pope, the Jews, and all the sects. I will confess that it is true. I would rather forfeit my life or jeopardize my property and honor than disavow this. Wherever faith is genuine, it cannot hold its tongue; it would rather suffer death. Such faith will also confess God's Word before tyrants. To be sure, it will encounter all sorts of trials and temptations from the devil, as the martyrs amply demonstrate. (AE 22:392–93)

Again Luther:

Reason plays the game of blind man's bluff with God. It makes nothing but false moves and always misses Him in that it calls that "God" which is not God; and, conversely, fails to call Him God who is God. . . . It goes about the matter in this clumsy way, ascribing the name of God and divine honor to what it imagines to be God but never hitting upon the true God but rather on the devil or its own notion, which the devil controls. This is the reason why there is indeed a very great difference between knowing that God exists and knowing what or who God really is. The first truth human nature knows, and it is written in all hearts; the second only the Holy Spirit teaches. (St. L 14:859)

Again Luther:

Turks and Jews boast a lot about God and claim to have a better faith than we Christians. They say they cannot be wrong. *They say that they believe [Glaube] in one God, who created heaven and earth and everything else.* This kind of faith certainly can not be wrong, they think. Christ, however, here concludes: "He who hates Me, hates my Father." *Now, since Turks and Jews hate Christ and persecute His Word, they certainly also hate the God who has created heaven and earth. They do not believe [Glaube] in Him and they do not honor Him. For Christ is the same one God.* (St. L 13a, 1285).

Many other quotations could be provided from Luther's works that show, by an overwhelming preponderance of the evidence, that Luther did not actually believe, or assert, without careful qualification and distinction, that Muslims, Jews, heathens, and other unbelievers do believe in and worship the one true God.

The Lutheran Confessions on the Issue of Who Knows God

We believe that the sentence as we have translated it in LC II 66 supports, and does not contradict what the Lutheran Confessions teach elsewhere. Note especially Luther's own remarks in the Lutheran Confessions, particularly from the Large Catechism. Permit us now to provide several quotations from the Lutheran Confessions.

The Lutheran Confessions:

> The ancient definition of original sin is that it is a lack of righteousness. This definition not only denies that mankind is capable of obedience in his body, but also denies that mankind is capable of knowing God, placing confidence in God, fearing and loving God, and certainly also the ability to produce such things. (Ap II 23)

Again, the Confessions:

> When we are born, we bring with us ignorance of God, unbelief, distrust, contempt, and hatred of God. (Ap II 29)

Again, the Confessions:

> Without the Holy Spirit human hearts have neither the fear of God nor trust in God nor the faith that God hears, forgives, helps, or saves them. Therefore they are *ungodly*; for "a bad tree cannot bear good fruit" (Matt 7:18) and

"without faith it is impossible to please" God (Heb 11:6). (Tappert, p. 225).

Again, the Confessions, from the Large Catechism:

As I have often said, the trust and faith of the heart alone make both God and an idol. If your faith and trust are right, then your God is the true God. On the other hand, if your trust is false and wrong, then you have not the true God. (Tappert, p. 365)

Again, the Confessions, from the Large Catechism:

On the other hand, you can easily judge how *the world practices nothing but false worship and idolatry*. There has never been a people so wicked that it did not establish and maintain some sort of worship. Everyone has set up a god of his own, to which he looked for blessings, help, and comfort. . . . Everyone made into a god that to which his heart was inclined. *Even in the mind of all the heathen, therefore, to have a god means to trust and believe. The trouble is that their trust is false and wrong, for it is not founded upon the one God, apart from whom there is truly no god in heaven or on earth. Accordingly the heathen actually fashion their fancies and dreams about God into an idol and entrust themselves to an empty nothing.* So it is with all idolatry. *Idolatry does not consist merely of erecting an image and praying to it. It is primarily in the heart*, which pursues other things and seeks help and consolation from creatures, saints, or devils. It neither cares for God nor expects good things from him sufficiently to trust that he wants to help, nor does it believe that whatever good it receives comes from God. (Tappert, pp. 366–77)

Again, the Confessions, from the Large Catechism:

Of this community (the church) I also am a part and member, a participant and co-partner in all the blessings it possesses. I was brought to it by the Holy Spirit and incorporated into it through the fact that I have heard and still hear God's Word, which is the first step in entering it. *Before we had advanced this far, we were entirely of the devil, knowing nothing of God and of Christ.* (Tappert, p. 417)

Again, the Confessions, from the Large Catechism:

Where the heart is not right with God and cannot achieve such confidence, it will never dare to pray. But such a confident and joyful heart can only come from the knowledge that our sins are forgiven. (Tappert, pp. 432–33)

Again, the Confessions, from the Large Catechism:

Whoever knows that in Christ he has a gracious God, truly knows God, calls upon him, and *is not, like the heathen, without God.* For the devil and the ungodly do not believe this article concerning the forgiveness of sin, and *so they are at enmity with God, cannot call upon him,* and have no hope of receiving good from him. (Tappert, p. 44)

Again, the Confessions:

For Pagans had something of a knowledge of God from the law of nature, but at the same *time they did not truly know him nor did they truly honor him* (Rom. 1[:19–32]). (Kolb and Wengert [K/W], p. 585)

The sentence in LC II 66 does not contradict the other clear statements in the Lutheran Confessions, particularly not in the Large Catechism itself. It is perfectly in line with what is said elsewhere in the Lutheran Confessions. Unbelievers do not know the true God. They do not actually pray to Him. They do not actually worship Him. They do not actually believe in Him. The Lutheran Confessions make it very clear that there is actually no belief and no worship of God, not even true knowledge of God, apart from, and without, Jesus Christ. While unbelievers may claim to believe and worship the true God, it is false faith and false worship, no real belief or worship at all. It sends people to hell for all eternity.

HOLY SCRIPTURE ON WHO KNOWS, BELIEVES, AND WORSHIPS THE ONE, TRUE GOD

God's Word teaches that only those who are brought to faith in Christ by the Holy Spirit believe in and worship one true God.

Then Jesus, still teaching in the temple courts, cried out, "Yes, you know me, and you know where I am from. I am not here on my own, but he who sent me is true. *You do not know him*, but I know him because I am from him and he sent me." (Jn 7:28–29)

Again, Holy Scripture:

"Then they asked him, "Where is your father?" "*You do not know me or my Father*," Jesus replied. "If you knew me, you would know my Father also." (Jn 8:19)

Again, Holy Scripture:

"We are not illegitimate children," they protested. "The only Father we have is God himself." Jesus said to them, *"If God were your Father, you would love me, for I came from God and now am here.* I have not come on my own; but he sent me. Why is my language not clear to you? Because you are unable to hear what I say. *You belong to your father, the devil, and you want to carry out your father's desire.*" (Jn 8:41)

Again, Holy Scripture:

Righteous Father, though the world does not know you, I know you. (Jn 17:25)

Again, Holy Scripture:

How, then, can they call on the one *they have not believed in? And how can they believe in the one of whom they have not heard?* And how can they hear without someone preaching to them? And how can they preach unless they are sent? As it is written, "How beautiful are the feet of those who bring good news!" (Rom 10:14–15)

Again, Holy Scripture:

> The *man without the Spirit does not accept the things that come from the Spirit* of God, for they are foolishness to him, and *he cannot understand them*, because they are spiritually discerned. (1 Cor 2:14)

Again, Holy Scripture:

> Formerly, *when you did not know God, you were slaves to those who by nature are not gods.* But now that you know God—or rather are known by God—how is it that you are turning back to those weak and miserable principles? Do you wish to be enslaved by them all over again? (Gal 4:8–9)

Again, Holy Scripture:

> Therefore, remember that formerly you who are Gentiles by birth and called "uncircumcised" by those who call themselves "the circumcision" (that done in the body by the hands of men) remember that *at that time you were separate from Christ, excluded from citizenship in Israel and foreigners to the covenants of the promise, without hope and without God in the world.* But now in Christ Jesus you who once were far away have been brought near through the blood of Christ. (Eph 2:11–13)

Again, Holy Scripture:

> It is God's will that you should be sanctified: that you should avoid sexual immorality; that each of you should learn to control his own body in a way that is holy and honorable, not in passionate lust *like the heathen, who do not know God.* (1 Thess 4:3–5)

Again, Holy Scripture:

> Who is the liar? It is the man who denies that Jesus is the Christ. Such a man is the antichrist—he denies the Father

and the Son. *No one who denies the Son has the Father; whoever acknowledges the Son has the Father also.* (1 Jn 2:22–23)

Again, Holy Scripture:

How great is the love the Father has lavished on us, that we should be called children of God! And that is what we are! *The reason the world does not know us is that it did not know him.* (1 Jn 3:1)

Again, Holy Scripture:

Dear friends, do not believe every spirit, but test the spirits to see whether they are from God, because many false prophets have gone out into the world. This is how you can recognize the Spirit of God: *Every spirit that acknowledges that Jesus Christ has come in the flesh is from God, but every spirit that does not acknowledge Jesus is not from God.* This is the spirit of the antichrist, which you have heard is coming and even now is already in the world. (1 Jn 4:1–3)

Again, Holy Scripture:

We are from God, and *whoever knows God listens to us*; but *whoever is not from God does not listen to us.* This is how we recognize the Spirit of truth and the spirit of falsehood. (1 Jn 4:6)

Again, Holy Scripture:

We know that we are children of God, and that the whole world is under the control of the evil one. We know also that the Son of God has come and has given us understanding, so that we may know him who is true. And we are in him who is true—even in his Son Jesus Christ. He is the true God and eternal life. Dear children, keep yourselves from idols. (1 Jn 5:19–20)

CONCLUSION

In light of the evidence from Luther's other writings, the Lutheran Confessions and Holy Scripture, we respectfully submit to the Commission on Doctrinal Review that the sentence as it reads presently in *Concordia: The Lutheran Confessions* is not contrary to Holy Scripture and the Lutheran Confessions:

> *Even if we conceded that everyone outside Christianity—whether heathen, Turk, Jews, or false Christians and hypocrites—believe in and worship only one true God, it would still be true that they do not know what His mind toward them is and cannot expect any love or blessing from Him.*

Christians alone believe in and worship the one, true God. Non-Christians, such as Turks and heathens, cannot worship the one true God because they do not believe in the Son of God, through whom alone we have access to the Father.

And so, while we believe our translation is sound, even if we were to concede that it is inaccurate, we do not believe that it advances false doctrine. We do believe, however, that the translation of LC II 66 that appears in *Concordia* accurately presents Luther's point and allows the reader of English more clearly and fully to understand what Luther is saying and what he is not saying.

Respectfully submitted,

Rev. Paul T. McCain
July 8, 2005

APPENDICES

Appendix A

LUTHER'S SERMON FROM MAY 23, 1528

The text that follows is a translation of WA XXX I, p. 9f. Not many copies of these sermon notes have been translated because earlier scholarship had wondered about their reliability. Aland and other recent scholars have overturned that opinion and now regard the sermon notes as reliable. See "Fragments and Crumbs for the Preachers" by Paul T. McCain in *Logia: A Journal of Lutheran Theology* (IX, no. 2 [2000]: 19–21).

Rörer's notes are macaronic, mostly Latin with some German. The three sermon series in WA XXX I are regarded as the sermons from which Luther created the Large Catechism. This sermon is the basis for Luther's comments in LC II 63–66, since there are significant points of contact between the two texts. The following notes will demonstrate this. The other sermons on the Creed in WA XXX I do not directly address the relationship between Christianity and other religions.

In the Ten Commandments[1] you hear, what kind of good works are commanded and which evil works are forbidden. Whoever would keep the Ten Commandments will do nothing evil, etc. We will [now][2] consider how we should rightly understand what [this statement] is: "I believe in God the Father" etc.[3]

Now [suppose] someone were to ask: "What kind of God do you have? What do you expect from Him? Since the gods of the pagans[4] and of the Jews are so diverse, do you also boast of your God, that He gave the Ten Commandments to you?"[5] The Creed serves this [purpose and explains]: That's who He is, that's how He's named, that's what He does, etc.

The Ten Commandments say nothing except, "You shall not have . . ." etc. Even the Jews and pagans confess this. But which of the two is true God—theirs or ours?[6] Then comes our Creed[7] and leaves nothing out, because it concerns our faith, that is: The Christian Faith.

Three times we say: "I believe" etc. First, it is said: "Father, Creator of heaven and earth" etc. Other gods, who did not establish heaven and earth, are not gods. Here the Jew and Turk respond: "I know this as well as you do."[8] Therefore the Christian adds [next]: "And in Jesus Christ" etc. Beyond this [fact] (that God created heaven and earth), He likewise has a Son, who is equally God, as is His Father. Here the Turks, Heathens, and Jews are divided from the Christians.[9] None is to be trusted nor believed except God alone. What kind of God is this Jesus Christ? He is "our Lord . . . conceived by the Holy Spirit." I mean, it may be said clearly enough[10] what kind of God [He is]. Only Christians believe this, not Jews, Turks, etc. Third, "In the Holy Spirit." If [He] is also God, what does He do? The Father created etc., the Son reconciled, the Holy Spirit acts, so that there is the Christian Church throughout the whole world, there is the forgiveness of sins, etc.

So the Creed is nothing other than an answer to this question: what kind [of God] is your God, who brought the Ten Commandments to you? By this faith we are separated from all other people,[11] who do not have it [this faith],[12] because they have another god, etc.[13]

If any person would have a god and would not know his name, power, etc., that would be a great shame, etc. The pagans attributed their god to any work.[14] Through this it is shown: whoever would declare [that he has] a god, must [also] declare what [the god] can do and is able to do. The Jews respond, when they are asked, what kind [of god] is their god: He who-they said[15]—created heaven and earth and led our fathers out of Egypt. So we [say]: "The nature of our God is that He created heaven and earth, and He has a Son, whom He sent into the world to become Man from a virgin, who also died for our sins, etc. The Father created all things, Christ redeemed us from all evil, the Holy Spirit rules through His Word and gives various gifts to the Church."

Are not these excellent works? Is not our God great, who created heaven, earth, and all things, who then is able to redeem us with His blood, who finally produces united faith and doctrine, [and] who will rouse the dead?

The heathen [can] only object that we make three gods. So the Creed, first, must be understood simply. Then consider the parts. Your God is Creator of heaven and earth, therefore all things are yours. The first commandment[16] teaches that God must be called upon in bad times and God must be trusted. At this point you hear He is able to fulfill all things that are asked of Him. Heaven gives the rain, the earth [gives] fruit, the sea [gives] fish, etc. He gives all these things because they are His. And furthermore, He is able and willing to redeem you from all evil. He did not create heaven and earth so that He should have [them], but it is announced to me and to you, that He created all things so that you might think: "If my God is so powerful, what will the pope do to me, [or] the devil and all his angels? They will not destroy the world because our God is more mighty."[17]

NOTES

1. The previous sermons were on the Ten Commandments.
2. Words supplied for the sake of clarity and smoother English are placed in brackets. In the American Edition of *Luther's Works*, such brackets would be removed in most cases, so as not to trouble the reader.

3. The notes frequently have "u" for "und so weiter," here represented by "etc." In most cases this could be left out.
4. Latin has "Gentiles."
5. Much of this sermon is written in the rhetorical form of a friendly dialogue between a Christian and a non-Christian (cf. Justin Martyr's "Dialogue with Trypho"). For LC II 63–66, he wrote in a different style. It has the form of a dialectical argument or dispute and is expressed more sharply through numerous all-inclusive and exclusive terms.
6. The sermon addresses three basic questions: (1) What is the purpose of the Creed? (2) How is this confession different from other confessions? (3) What are God's works?
7. Literally, "faith." Here translated as "Creed" since in German (the language in which he was preaching) "*Glaube*" is the term for the Creed.
8. Quotation marks are supplied at points in order to make the dialogue clearer for the English reader.
9. "Da scheiden sich Turken, Heiden, Juden a Christianis." Similar words are used in LC II 66 to describe how "these articles of the Creed divide and separate us Christians from all other people on earth." In this sermon Luther describes non-Christian groups but does not refer to "false Christians and hypocrites" as he does in LC II 66b.
10. Luther uses a similar idiom in the Large Catechism. It literally says, "It may be said in German well enough."
11. Cf. wording in LC II 66.
12. Or, "do not have the Creed."
13. Luther was explaining that even though Christians, Jews, and others may use the same words and make similar claims, they did not have the same confession of faith and therefore did not have the same God. Cf. his explanation of the First Commandment in the Large Catechism.
14. "Gentiles dederunt cuilibet operi suum deum." An idiom is involved.
15. Note how Luther qualifies their statement. They claim the Creator, but Luther does not allow that they actually have Him as their God. Cf. the Latin text of LC II 66b, which uses an ACI construction, "Even if they believe that there is only one true God and call on Him."
16. Luther refers to the commandment, "You shall not misuse the name of the Lord your God" and his explanation.
17. Three more short paragraphs describe God's works.

Appendix B

LUTHER'S *PER IMPOSSIBILE* SENTENCES

Luther frequently used dialectical reasoning in his writings or described dialectical reasoning in the writings of others. For example, in his comments on 1 Corinthians 15, Luther described Paul's use of a *reductio ad impossibile* argument:

> [Paul] makes proper use of that device of dialectics which is known as *reducere per impossible*. He wants to say: "Whoever denies this article must simultaneously deny far more, namely, first of all, that you believe properly; in the second place, that the Word which you believe has been true; in the third place, that we apostles preach correctly and that we are God's apostles; in the fourth place, that God is truthful; in brief, that God is God. (AE 28:95)

As a student Luther would have written *per impossibile* sentences for dialectical exercises. He would have included the actual dialectical term as part of the sentence, even though the sentences did not require them.

Luther continued to use this grammar school practice in his later writing. Examples follow, extending from 1517 to 1545. They illustrate the various structures of *per impossibile* sentences. In some cases (21.4 percent of examples here) Luther placed the concessive clause at the end of the sentence.[1] But in most cases (78.6 percent) Luther places the concession first, followed by its conclusion.[2] This is the construction he used in LC II 66b.

> To consider papal indulgences so great that they could absolve a man even if he *had done the impossible* and had violated the mother of God is madness. (AE 31:240; 1517)

> But the children of God do good with a will that is disinterested, not seeking any reward, but only the glory and will of God, and being ready to do good even if—*an impossible supposition*—there were neither a kingdom nor a hell. (AE 33:152–53; 1525)

> And it is no small comfort to know that one is pleasing to God, even if there were nothing else to follow from it, *though that is impossible.* (AE 33:154; 1525)

> If God foreknows that Judas will turn traitor, or that he will change his will to betray, whichever God has foreknown will necessarily come about, or else God will be mistaken in his foreknowing and predicting, *which is impossible.* (AE 33:194–95; 1525)

> But one thing more: even though they should produce such an example in one passage of Scripture (*which, however, is impossible*), they are still under obligation to prove that it is necessarily so here in the Supper as well, that "body" is "sign of the body." (AE 37:35; 1527)

> Even if one could interpret the gospels as applying only to priests, *which is a sheer impossibility*, one would still run up against St. Paul in I Corinthians 11 [:23–30], where the sacrament is given to all Christians in Corinth and Paul upbraids them for their abuse of it, saying that many were ill and had died from unworthy eating and drinking of the sacrament. (AE 43:152; 1527)

> Even if God could be appeased (*which is impossible*), He could never be appeased by our works, because these are far too small. To appease God we should have to offer Him works of equal value. (AE 17:24; ca. 1527)

For though they should know and understand it perfectly (*which, however, is impossible in this life*), yet there are manifold benefits and fruits still to be obtained, if it be daily read and practised in thought and speech. (*Triglotta*, LC Preface 9; 1529)

For (as we have said) even though infants did not believe, *which, however, is not the case*, yet their baptism as now shown would be valid, and noone should rebaptize them. (*Triglotta*, LC IV 55; 1529)

Supposing, I say, that the Pope and See at Rome would yield and accept this (*which, nevertheless, is impossible . . .*), nevertheless, even in this way Christianity would not be helped, but many more sects would arise than before. (*Triglotta*, SA II IV 7; 1537)

Even if we would assume—*which is impossible*—that the seventy weeks began with the destruction of Jerusalem, we could still not justify this stupid lie. (AE 47:247; 1543)

Even if *the impossible* were true, and they were right that mere bread and wine are in the Lord's Supper, should they for that reason rage and thunder thus against us with such hideous blasphemies, "baked God," "God of bread," etc.? (AE 38:295; 1544)

Otherwise, if this attitude should obtain that it does not harm anyone if he desires to deny one article of the faith because he still regards all the others as true (although basically *this is impossible*), then no heretic would ever be condemned, indeed, there could not even be a heretic on earth. (AE 38:308; 1544)

And even if he had had them—*which is impossible, and to which the other apostles and Christ say no*—the bishop of Rome could still not be St. Peter's only heir. (AE 41:351; 1545)

Example number	Reference	Concessive conjunction	Concessive form	All-inclusive or exclusive terms	Conclusion formula	Verb mood
Imp 1	AE 31:240; WA 1:622; 1518	etiam siquis; even if	condition-conclusion			Subjunctive; violasset
Imp 2	AE 33:153; WA 18:694; 1525	si; even if	conclusion-condition	neque . . . neque		Subjunctive; esset
Imp 3	AE 33:154; WA 18:695; 1525	ut; even if	conclusion-condition	nihil aliud		Subjunctive; sequatur
Imp 4	AE 33:194–95; WA 18:722; 1525	si; if	conclusion-condition			Indicative?; praescit
Imp 5	AE 37:35; WA 23:97; 1527	wenn . . . gleich; even though	condition-conclusion	einem	so . . . dennoch auch	Subjunctive?; auffbreckten
Imp 6	AE 43:152; WA 23:414; 1527	wenn . . . gleich; even if	condition-conclusion	alleine	so . . . doch . . . nicht	Subjunctive; kunde
Imp 7	AE 17:24; WA 31 II:279; ca. 1527	eciam si; even if	condition-conclusion		tamen	Subjunctive; possit
Imp 8	Same as CC1 LC pref. 9; pp. 568–69; 1529	ob . . . gleich; though	condition-conclusion	allerdings . . . allerbeste; negation clause added; doch nicht	so . . . doch	Subjunctive; wüssten und könnten

Example number	Reference	Concessive conjunction	Concessive form	All-inclusive or exclusive terms	Conclusion formula	Verb mood
Imp 9	Same as CC42 LC IV 55; pp. 744–45; 1529	wenngleich; even though	condition-conclusion	negation clause added doch nicht	so . . . doch	Subjunctive; glaubten
Imp 10	SA II IV 7; 1537	ich setze nun; supposing	condition-conclusion	negation clause added;		Subjunctive; begeben und annehmen wollte
Imp 11	AE 47:247; WA 53:506; 1543	wenn . . . gleich; even if	condition-conclusion		so . . . doch nicht	Indicative or subjunctive; setzen
Imp 12	AE 38:295; WA 54:147; 1544	wens; even if	condition-conclusion			Subjunctive; war . . . hetten
Imp 13	AE 38:308; WA 54:158; 1544	sonst . . . wo; otherwise, if	condition-conclusion	einem . . . alle	so . . . nimmer	Indicative with auxiliary; solt gelten
Imp 14	AE 41:351; WA 54:278; 1545	wenn . . . gleich; even if	condition-conclusion		dennoch . . . nicht	Subjunctive; gehabt hette

NOTES

1. All such examples are from the "The Bondage of the Will." Perhaps Luther chose this particular grammatical form for his dispute with Erasmus.
2. In "The Bondage of the Will" Luther described some examples of sentences that automatically imply *per impossibile* reasoning. Note his use of sarcasm in the examples. "By what sort of logic, I ask you, does it follow that the will and the ability must be present as soon as it is said, 'If you will, if any man will, if you are willing'? Do we not very often use such expressions to signify instead impotence and impossibility? For instance: 'If you wish to equal Virgil in singing, my dear Maevius, you must sing other songs!'; 'If you, Scotus, want to surpass Cicero, you will have to replace your sophistries with consummate eloquence'; 'If you wish to be compared with David, you must write psalms like his.' Here it is obvious that the things mentioned are impossible as far as our own powers are concerned, though they could all be done by divine power. That is how it is in the Scriptures too; there also expressions like these are used in order to show what can be done in us by the power of God, and what we cannot do ourselves." (AE 33:148)

Appendix C

THE SQUARE OF OPPOSITIONS

The square of oppositions was a standard tool in medieval dialectic. It was based on Aristotle's *On Interpretation*. The illustration below is from Melanchthon's textbook on dialectic, *Erotemata Dialectices* (1520), which is found in CR XIII:585.

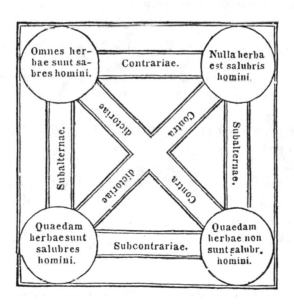

Students would use the square to guide them in forming arguments and syllogisms. Each corner of the square corresponded with different argumentative terms, based on the medieval philosophy of universals and particulars:

- Upper left: All
- Upper right: None
- Bottom left: Some
- Bottom right: Some not

The branches from the corners described the relationship between the arguments. The texts in the corners of Melanchthon's example state the following:

- Upper left: All plants are healthy for people.
- Upper right: No plant is healthy for people.
- Bottom left: Some plants are healthy for people.
- Bottom right: Some plants are not healthy for people.

In general, medieval thinkers believed that a properly written syllogism proved that something was true. Students were constantly drilled in these exercises. They wrote and defended theses (disputations) using these tools of argument.

LUTHER'S ARGUMENT IN THE LARGE CATECHISM

Luther's opponent in LC II 66 began his argument at the bottom left corner of the square:

Some people outside Christianity believe in and worship only one true God.

This was the position of writers like Erasmus and the Swiss Reformers such as Ulrich Zwingli. The argument implied that if such people believe in the one true God, they have salvation from Him. In contradiction, Luther's belief stood at the upper right hand corner of the square:

No one outside Christianity believes in and worships only one true God.

Luther's argument implied that everyone outside Christianity was outside the promised blessings of salvation because they did not truly have the right God (LC I:1–4; see also Appendix A).

Luther wanted to show the flaws in his opponent's belief. To illustrate and amplify the problems, Luther wrote a *per impossibile* argument. He granted a concession by moving the opponent's argument to the upper left corner of the square:

[What if we grant that:] All people outside of Christianity believe in and worship only one true God.

Luther then demonstrated that, even with this most generous concession, none of the people outside Christianity would have (1) knowledge of God's mind toward them, (2) any hope for God's blessings, (3) the Lord Christ, or (4) the gifts of the Holy Spirit. They would still be lost. This test revealed the numerous problems with the opponent's argument.

Appendix D

A CHART OF
CONCESSIVE CLAUSES

Luther was especially fond of the dialectical and rhetorical power of concessive constructions. The following chart presents fifty-nine concessive clauses Luther used in the Large Catechism (1529) and the Smalcald Articles (1537). The references and texts are drawn from the *Concordia Triglotta*. The chart includes all clauses beginning with *ob ... gleich; obgleich; wenn ... gleich; or wenngleich*. These forms were chosen to provide context for Luther's use of the *ob ... gleich* construction in LC II 66b. The key clauses for this comparison are in bold. This is not an exhaustive list of Luther's concessive constructions.

Example number	Reference	Concessive conjunction	Concessive form	All-inclusive or exclusive terms	Conclusion formula	Verb mood
CC1	LC pref. 9; pp. 568–69	ob . . . gleich; even though	conclusion-condition	allzu wohl		subjunctive or indicative; dünkt
CC2	**LC pref. 9; pp. 568–69**	**ob . . . gleich; though**	**condition-conclusion**	**allerdings . . . allerbeste; negation clause added; doch nicht**	**so . . . doch**	**subjunctive; wüssten und könnten**
CC3	LC I 26; pp. 586–87	ob . . . gleich; even though	condition-conclusion		so . . . doch	indicative; widerfährt
CC4	**LC I 36; pp. 588–89**	**ob . . . gleich; although**	**condition-conclusion**		**so . . . doch . . . nicht**	**subjunctive or indicative; findet**
CC5	LC I 43; pp. 590–91	ob . . . gleich; even though	condition-conclusion		doch	past particle; indicative or subjunctive; [ge]bracht
CC6	**LC I 91; pp. 606–7**	**ob . . . gleich; though**	**condition-conclusion**	**aller**	**so . . . doch . . . nichts**	**subjunctive; hätten**
CC7	LC I 100; pp. 606–7	ob . . . gleich; even though	condition-conclusion	beste . . . aller	so . . . doch	subjunctive; könntest

Example number	Reference	Concessive conjunction	Concessive form	All-inclusive or exclusive terms	Conclusion formula	Verb mood
CC8	LC I 101; pp. 608–9	ob ... gleich; even though	condition-conclusion	kein anderer	so ... doch	subjunctive; triebe
CC9	LC I 108; pp. 610–611	ob ... gleich; however	condition-conclusion;		dass ... dennoch	subjunctive; seien
CC10	LC I 110; pp. 610–13	ob ... gleich; even though	conclusion-condition			indicative; tun
CC11	LC I 117; pp. 614–15	ob ... gleich; although	conclusion-condition	aller- (prefix)		passive infinitive; angesehen wird
CC12	LC I 120; pp. 614–15	ob ... gleich; even though	conclusion-condition			subjunctive or indicative; fastert und ... beten
CC13	LC I 176; pp. 630–31	ob ... gleich; even though	conclusion-condition			subjunctive; wärest
CC14	LC I 186; pp. 632–33	ob ... gleich; even though	conclusion-condition	höchlich		subjunctive; verdient

Example number	Reference	Concessive conjunction	Concessive form	All-inclusive or exclusive terms	Conclusion formula	Verb mood
CC15	LC I 215; pp. 640–41	ob . . . gleich; even though	condition-conclusion		so . . . doch	subjunctive or indicative; enthalten
CC16	**LC I 216; pp. 640–41**	**ob . . . gleich; even if**	**condition-conclusion**		**doch nicht**	**subjunctive; wäre**
CC17	LC I 265; pp. 656–57	ob . . . gleich; although	conclusion-condition			indicative; sieht
CC18	LC I 269; pp. 656–57	wenn . . . gleich; even though	conclusion-condition			indicative; ist
CC19	**LC I 270; pp. 656–57**	**ob . . . gleich; although**	**condition-conclusion; within subordinate clause**		**so . . . doch . . . nicht**	**indicative; ist**
CC20	LC I 296; pp. 664–65	ob . . . gleich; even though	conclusion-condition			subjunctive or indicative; kommen kann
CC21	LC I 307; pp. 668–69	ob . . . gleich; even if	conclusion-condition			modal verb (possibility); behalten kannst
CC22	LC I 307; pp. 668–69	ob . . . gleich; although	condition-conclusion	niemand	so . . . doch	indicative; hingehst
CC23	LC I 328; pp. 674–75	ob . . . gleich; even though	conclusion-condition	kein mensch		subjunctive; hättest . . . strafte

Example number	Reference	Concessive conjunction	Concessive form	All-inclusive or exclusive terms	Conclusion formula	Verb mood
CC24	LC II 55; pp. 692–93	ob . . . gleich; although	condition-conclusion		doch . . . nicht	subjunctive or indicative; haben
CC25	LC II 66; pp. 696–97	ob . . . gleich; although	condition-conclusion	nur	so . . . doch . . . nicht	subjunctive or indicative; glauben . . . anbeten
CC26	LC III 2; pp. 696–97	ob . . . gleich; even though	condition-conclusion; within subordinate clause		nichts so	indicative; angefangen hat zu glauben
CC27	LC III 11; pp. 700–701	ob . . . gleich; although	conclusion-condition			sind
CC28	LC III 63; pp. 714–15	ob . . . gleich; even though	conclusion-condition			subjunctive or indicative; angenommen haben . . . glauben
CC29	LC III 74; pp. 718–19	ob . . . gleich; though	condition-conclusion	aller	so . . . doch . . . keines	subjunctive or indicative; überkommen haben
CC30	LC III 86; pp. 722–23	ob . . . gleich; although	condition-conclusion; within subordinate clause		doch . . . nicht	subjunctive or indicative; haben

Example number	Reference	Concessive conjunction	Concessive form	All-inclusive or exclusive terms	Conclusion formula	Verb mood
CC31	LC III 100; pp. 724–25	ob . . . gleich; although	condition-conclusion	ganz	so . . . doch	subjunctive or indicative; überkommen haben; losgesprochen sind
CC32	LC IV 10; pp. 734–35	ob . . . gleich; although	condition-conclusion		so . . . doch	indicative; geschieht
CC33	**LC IV 12; pp. 734–35**	**wenn . . . gleich; even though**	**condition-conclusion**	**aller**	**so . . . doch nicht**	**subjunctive; schlüge**
CC34	LC IV 30; pp. 738–39	ob . . . gleich; though	conclusion-condition			indicative; ist
CC35	LC IV 34; pp. 740–41	ob . . . gleich; notwithstanding	conclusion-condition			indicative; ist
CC36	LC IV 38; pp. 740–41	ob . . . gleich; though	conclusion-condition	ganz		indicative; ist
CC37	LC IV 43; pp. 742–43	ob . . . gleich; even though	condition-conclusion			subjunctive; stürben
CC38	LC IV 53; pp. 744–45	ob . . . gleich; even though	conclusion-condition			passive infinitive; gebraucht wird

APPENDIX D

Example number	Reference	Concessive conjunction	Concessive form	All-inclusive or exclusive terms	Conclusion formula	Verb mood
CC39	**LC IV 54; pp. 744–45**	**wenn gleich; even though**	**condition-conclusion**		**nichts-desto-weniger**	**indicative; herzukäme; tauften**
CC40	LC IV 54; pp. 744–45	ob . . . gleich; even though	conclusion-condition			indicative; empfängt
CC41	LC IV 54; pp. 744–45	ob . . . gleich; even though	conclusion-condition			subjunctive or indicative; glauben
CC42	**LC IV 55; pp. 744–45**	**wenngleich; even though**	**condition-conclusion**	**negation clause added; doch nicht**	**so . . . doch**	**subjunctive; glaubten**
CC43	LC IV 59; pp. 746–47	ob . . . gleich; though	conclusion-condition			indicative; trägt
CC44	LC IV 60; pp. 746–47	wenngleich; even though	conclusion-condition	nur		subjunctive; getauft würde
CC45	LC IV 78; pp. 750–51	ob . . . gleich; even though	condition-conclusion	hundertmal	doch immer	subjunctive; ließe
CC46	LC IV 86; pp. 752–53	ob . . . gleich; even though	condition-conclusion		Also	subjunctive or indicative; sündigen

129

Example number	Reference	Concessive conjunction	Concessive form	All-inclusive or exclusive terms	Conclusion formula	Verb mood
CC47	LC V 5; pp. 752–55	ob . . . gleich; although	condition-conclusion	nimmermehr		ind/subj [?]; hältst; betest; glaubst
CC48	LC V 5; pp. 754–55	ob . . . gleich; even though	conclusion-condition			subjunctive or indicative; [ge]brauchen und handeln
CC49	LC V 16; pp. 756–57	ob . . . gleich; even though	condition-conclusion		so	indicative; nimmet oder gibt
CC50	LC V 16; pp. 756–57	ob . . . gleich; even though	conclusion-condition			passive infinitive; missbraucht wird
CC51	LC V 59; pp. 766–67	ob . . . gleich; even though	conclusion-condition			indicative; sind
CC52	SA II II 6; pp. 462–63	wenn . . . gleich; even though	conclusion-condition			subjunctive; hätte
CC53	SA II II 22; pp. 468–69	wenngleich; even though	conclusion-condition			subjunctive; wäre
CC54	SA II II 25; pp. 468–69	wenn . . . gleich; even though	conclusion-condition	negation clause added; als doch nicht		subjunctive; wäre

Example number	Reference	Concessive conjunction	Concessive form	All-inclusive or exclusive terms	Conclusion formula	Verb mood
CC55	**SA II IV 4; pp. 472–73**	**wenn . . . gleich; although**	**condition-conclusion**	alles	**so . . . doch nichts**	**indicative; glaubst . . . hast**
CC56	SA II IV 9; pp. 472–73	ob . . . wohl ungleich; although	conclusion-conditio; parenthetical statement			indicative or subjunctive; [sind or seien]
CC57	**SA III VI 3; pp. 492–93**	**ob . . . gleich; even if**	**condition-conclusion**		**so . . . doch nicht**	**subjunctive; wäre**
CC58	SA III VIII 4; pp. 494–95	wenn . . . gleich; even though	conclusion-condition			indicative; ist
CC59	SA III VIII 7; pp. 494–95	ob . . . gleich; even though	conclusion-condition			indicative or subjunctive; [sind or seien]; kriegen

Appendix E

TRANSLATIONS OF
LUTHER'S CLAUSES

A variety of English translations for the Large Catechism have been made since the nineteenth century. They include the following:

The Christian Book of Concord. Newmarket: Solomon D. Henkel and Bros., 1851.
Concordia: The Lutheran Confessions. St. Louis: CPH, 2005.
Dau, W. H. T., and F. Bente, eds. Concordia Triglotta. St. Louis: CPH, 1921.
Jacobs, Henry E., ed. The Book of Concord. Vol. 1. Philadelphia: Board of Publications of the General Council of the Evangelical Lutheran Church in North America, 1908.
Janzow, F. Samuel, trans. Luther's Large Catechism. St. Louis: CPH, 1978.
Kolb, Robert, and Timothy J. Wengert, eds. The Book of Concord. Minneapolis: Fortress, 2000.
Lenker, John Nicholas, trans. Luther's Large Catechism. Minneapolis: The Luther Press, 1908.
Tappert, Theodore G., ed. Book of Concord. Philadelphia: Fortress, 1959.

A survey of these translations demonstrates a tendency from the Jacobs edition[1] to provide ambiguous translations of some "*ob . . . gleich*" constructions—LC II 66b being a prime example.[2] The more recent translations (Tappert, Janzow, K/W, and *Concordia*) tend to represent Luther's constructions with "even if," in keeping with current English. Here is a tally based on final analysis of the verbs, structure, and content:

Tally for key examples (LC II 66 included)	
Indicative	4
Indicative or subjunctive	1
Subjunctive	9

Below are notes regarding some of the translations of the key examples from Appendix D, which most closely parallel LC II 66b. At the introduction to each passage, a description of the verb in the concessive clause is provided. The concessive clause is italicized in each translation. When the mood of the verb in the concessive clause was indicative—departing from the dominant form of these constructions —comments are added to explain why the indicative was used. Special emphasis is given to Luther's all-inclusive and exclusive terms, since they are so important for sharpening his rhetoric and dialectic (see Chapters 6 and 7).

CC2: Large Catechism, Preface 9 (subjunctive)
Henkel (1851): For let us make the most generous supposition;—*let us grant that they do remember and understand every principle to the utmost perfection,*—a thing which it is impossible to attain in this life,—yet we must never forget the endless applications and benefits resulting from a daily perusal of these same principles, and from daily exercise in meditating and discoursing upon them.
Jacobs (1882): For *though they should know and understand it perfectly* (which, however, is impossible in this life), yet if it be daily read and practiced in thought and speech, it yields much profit and fruit.
Lenker (1908): *Though their knowledge of these writings were perfect*, which is impossible in the present life, it would still be a highly profitable and useful exercise daily to read them and to make them the subject of meditation and conversation . . .
Triglotta (1921): For *though they should know and understand it perfectly* (which, however, is impossible in this life), yet there are manifold benefits and fruits still to be obtained, if it be daily read and practised in thought and speech . . .
Tappert (1959): *Even if their knowledge of the Catechism were perfect* (though that is impossible in this life), yet it is highly profitable and fruitful daily to read it and make it the subject of meditation and conversation.

Janzow (1928): *Even if their knowledge of the Catechism truths were perfect* (something that in this life is impossible), yet to read it daily and to make it the subject of one's thinking and conversation has all manner of practical results and brings fruitful rewards.

K/W (2000): *Even if their knowledge of the catechism were perfect* (although that is impossible in this life), yet it is highly profitable and fruitful to read it daily and to make it the subject of meditation and conversation.

Concordia (2005): For *even if they know and understand the catechism perfectly* (which, however, is impossible in this life), there are still many benefits and fruits to be gained, if it is daily read and practiced in thought and speech.

CC4: Large Catechism I 36 (indicative or subjunctive)

Henkel: Therefore, *although, at the present day, haughty, mighty, and opulent misers are found*, who insolently depend on their mammon, disregardful of God's being angry or not angry, as if they would without hesitation venture to withstand his wrath; yet they shall, however, not be able to accomplish it . . .

Jacobs: Therefore, *although proud, powerful and rich worldlings are now to be found*, . . . ; yet, before they are aware, they shall be wrecked . . .

Lenker: *There are still found proud, powerful, and rich bloats,* who defiantly boast of their mammon, unconcerned whether they provoke God to anger or to mirth.

Triglotta: *Although proud, powerful and rich worldlings . . . are now to be found* . . ., yet they shall not succeed . . .

Tappert: *Even now there are proud, powerful, and rich pot-bellies* who, not caring whether God frowns or smiles, boast defiantly of their mammon and believe that they can withstand his wrecked, along with all they have trusted in, just as all others have perished who thought themselves to be so high and mighty.

Janzow: *Today there are certain proud, powerful, rich maggots,* defiantly boastful of their mammon and not caring whether God smiles or frowns, who confidently expect to outlast the tempest of God's wrath.

K/W: *Even now there are proud, powerful, and rich potbellies* who, not caring whether God frowns or smiles, boast defiantly of their mammon and believe that they can withstand his wrath.

Concordia: *Proud, powerful, and rich men of the world* (Sardanapalians and Phalarides, who surpass even the Persians in wealth) *are still to be found.*

Note how translators, beginning with Lenker, have turned this concessive construction with an indicative verb into a declarative sentence. Also note that, even though the sentence starts with a declaration, Luther couples it with a hyperbolic description of the rich people's defiance toward God. He turns up the rhetoric and so naturally concludes the sentence with a negation. If Luther had added an exclusive term (e.g., "*only* rich worldlings are now to be found"), one would expect a subjunctive mood verb in the concessive clause.

CC6: Large Catechism I 91 (subjunctive)
Henkel: For *even if we had all the sainted relics, or holy and consecrated clothes together in a mass*, it would still benefit us nothing; for it is all a dead thing, which can sanctify no one.
Jacobs: For *though we had the bones of all the saints, or all holy and consecrated garments upon a heap*, they would not avail us anything; for all that is a dead thing which can sanctify nobody.
Lenker: *Although we were to gather in a heap the bones or the holy and consecrated garments of all the saints*, they could not help us; for they all are lifeless things that can sanctify no one.
Triglotta: For *though we had the bones of all the saints or all holy and consecrated garments upon a heap*, still that would help us nothing; for all that is a dead thing which can sanctify nobody.
Tappert: *Though we had the bones of all the saints or all the holy and consecrated vestments gathered together in one heap*, they could not help us in the slightest degree, for they are all dead things that can sanctify no one.
Janzow: For *even if we gathered into one heap the bones of all the saints together with all holy, consecrated vestments*, all these would not help us in the least. They are all dead things and cannot sanctify any one.
K/W: *Even if we had the bones of all the saints or all the holy and consecrated vestments gathered together in one pile*, they would not help us in the least, for they are all dead things that cannot make anyone holy.
Concordia: *Though we had the bones of all the saints or all holy and consecrated garments upon a heap*, still that would not help us at all. All that stuff is a dead thing that can sanctify no one.

CC16: Large Catechism I 216 (subjunctive)

Henkel: . . . for *even admitting that monastic life might be godly*, it still does not lie in their power to observe continence; and if they do continue in this observance, they must sin to a greater extent against this commandment.

Jacobs: . . . considering that *even if the monastic life had divine sanction*, it were nevertheless out of their power to maintain chastity, and if they remain in that condition they must only sin more and more against this commandment.

Lenker: *Even granting that cloister life is godly*, it is not in the power of the incumbents to observe continence, and if they remain they must sin only more and more against this commandment.

Triglotta: . . . considering that *even if the monastic life were godly*, it would nevertheless not be in their power to maintain chastity, and if they remain in it, they must only sin more and more against this commandment.

Tappert: *Even granting that the monastic life is godly*, yet it is not in their power to maintain chastity, and if they remain they will inevitably sin more and more against this commandment.

Janzow: . . . *even if their monastic life were godly in other respects*, yet the maintenance of chastity is beyond its power, and if they remain in monastic life, they will inevitably only sin all the more and all the longer against this commandment.

K/W: In this regard, *even if the monastic life were godly*, still it is not in their power to maintain chastity. If they remain in it, they will inevitably sin more and more against this commandment.

Concordia: They must consider that *even if the monastic life were godly*, it would still not be in their power to maintain chastity. And if they remain in their monastic vows, they must only sin more and more against this commandment.

CC19: Large Catechism I 270 (indicative)

Henkel: If you circulate it, *even if it be true*, you must still be regarded as a liar, because you are unable to make it appear true: and besides, you act like a wicked wretch, since no one has a right to speak injuriously of the honor and reputation of his fellow man, unless that honor and reputation have been already taken away from him by legal authority.

Jacobs: For if you repeat it, *although it be true*, you will appear as a liar, because you cannot prove it, and you are besides acting wickedly.

Lenker: If you spread a report which you are unable to prove, you must appear to be a liar.[3]

Triglotta: For if you tell it to others, *although it be true*, you will appear as a liar . . .

Tappert: For when you repeat a story that you cannot prove, *even if it is true*, you appear as a liar.

Janzow: For by repeating the story you will seem a liar *even if the story is true*, since you cannot prove it.

K/W: For when you repeat a story that you cannot prove, *even though it is true*, you appear as a liar.

Concordia: For if you tell the matter to others—*although it is true*—you will look like a liar, because you cannot prove it.

Note that the passage does not use any all-inclusive or exclusive terms. The mood of the verb is indicative but appears within a subordinate clause, making it hypothetical, which is how the translators treat it.

CC24: Large Catechism II 55 (indicative or subjunctive)

Henkel: Thus the Holy Ghost accomplishes this happy end for us, that, *even if we are contaminated with sins*, they still, however, cannot injure us, since we are in the Christian church . . .

Jacobs: Thus, *although we have sin*, the Holy Ghost does not allow it to injure us, because we are in the Christian Church, where there is full forgiveness of sin, both in that God forgives us, and in that we forgive, bear with and help each other.

Lenker: *Although we have sin*, it cannot harm us, because we are part of Christendom, where there is entire forgiveness of sins; God forgives us, and we forgive, bear with and help each other.

Triglotta: Thus, *although we have sins*, the [grace of the] Holy Ghost does not allow them to injure us . . .

Tappert: *Although we have sin*, the Holy Spirit sees to it that it does not harm us because we are in the Christian church, where there is full forgiveness of sin.

Janzow: What the Holy Spirit does for us is this: *although we have sin*, yet He orders things so that it cannot injure us because we are within the Christian community in which there is complete forgiveness of sins.

K/W: *Although we have sin*, the Holy Spirit sees to it that it does not harm us because we are a part of this Christian community.

Concordia: So *even though we have sins*, the grace of the Holy Spirit does not allow them to harm us.

This is a statement of fact. Note that this condition does not include any all-inclusive or exclusive terms. If it had (e.g., "even if we have *all* sins"), one would expect a subjunctive mood verb expressing a contrary-to-fact concession.

CC25: Large Catechism II 66 (indicative or subjunctive)

Henkel: For those who are not in the Christian church, no matter whether they be Pagans, Turks, Jews, or hypocrites, *even if they believe in and worship only one true God,* still do not know what his will toward them is . . .

Jacobs: For all outside of Christianity, whether heathen, Turks, Jews or false Christians and hypocrites, *although they believe in and worship only one true God,* yet know not what his mind toward them is . . .

Lenker: For all outside of Christendom, be they heathen, Turks, Jews, or false Christians and hypocrites, *even though they may believe in and worship only one true God,* do not know his mind toward them.

Triglotta: For all outside of Christianity, whether heathen, Turks, Jews, or false Christians and hypocrites, *although they believe in, and worship, only one true God,* yet know not what His mind towards them is . . .

Tappert: All who are outside the Christian Church, whether heathen, Turks, Jews, or false Christians and hypocrites, *even though they believe in and worship only the one, true God,* nevertheless do not know what his attitude is toward them.

Janzow: All those outside of the Christian community, be they heathen, Turks, Jews, or false Christians and hypocrites, *even though they believe in and worship only the one true God,* nevertheless do not know how He is disposed toward them.

K/W: All who are outside this Christian people, whether heathen, Turks, Jews, or false Christians and hypocrites—*even though they believe in and worship only the one, true God*—nevertheless do not know what his attitude toward them is.

Nordling (2003): *Even if it were the case . . . that they believe in, and worship, only true God . . .* [4]

Concordia: *Even if we were to concede that . . .* [they] *believe in and worship only one true God,* it would still be true that they do not know what His mind toward them is . . .

139

The Henkel translation uses "even if," moving the reader toward a contrary-to-fact interpretation. Lenker recognized the verbs as subjunctive, as shown by the word "may" in his translation. Nordling's article provides an idiomatic translation, using "were" to show that the verbs are subjunctive and that the clause is contrary to fact. *Concordia* represents the verbs as subjunctive with the word "were" and supplies "to concede" to show that the clause is a concession contrary to fact. Modern German editors also have chosen wording to represent the verbs as subjunctive or the clauses as contrary to fact. See note 7 in Chapter 10.

CC29: Large Catechism III 74 (subjunctive or indicative)

Henkel: For, *although we may have obtained an abundance of all kinds of good from God*, yet we are unable to preserve any of them, or to use them securely and joyfully, if he would not give us a permanent and a peaceful government.

Jacobs: For *although we had received of God all good things in abundance*, we should not be able to retain any of them, or use them in security and happiness, if he did not give us a permanent and peaceful government.

Lenker: *Although we receive from God all good things in abundance*, yet we are unable to retain any of them or to enjoy them in safety and happiness unless he gives us a stable and peaceful government.

Triglotta: For *though we have received of God all good things in abundance*, we are not able to retain any of them . . .

Tappert: *Although we have received from God all good things in abundance*, we cannot retain any of them or enjoy them in security and happiness unless he gives us a stable, peaceful government.

Janzow: For *although we have received from God an abundance of all good gifts*, yet we cannot retain any of them or enjoy them in happy security unless God grants us a stable and peaceable government.

K/W: *Although we have received from God all good things in abundance*, we cannot retain any of them or enjoy them in security and happiness were he not to give us a stable, peaceful government.

Concordia: *Though we have received from God all good things in abundance*, we are not able to keep any of them or use them in security and happiness if He did not give us a permanent and peaceful government.

The Henkel and Jacobs editions translate the clause with a subjunctive mood verb. This is the best choice, given the sharpness of the conclusion ("we are not able to retain *any* of them").

CC30: Large Catechism III 86 (subjunctive or indicative)
Henkel: This article touches our miserable and wretched life, which, *although we may have the word of God, we may believe, perform his will, and suffer, and nourish ourselves with the gifts and blessings of God,* does not, however, proceed without sin . . .
Jacobs: The point now pertains to our poor miserable life, which, *although we have and believed the Word of God, and do and suffer his will, and are supported by his gifts and blessings,* is nevertheless not without sin.
Lenker: *Although we have God's Word and believe and do God's will and submit to it, and though we are nourished by God's gifts and blessings,* our lives are not free from sin.
Triglotta: *Although we have and believe the Word of God, and do and submit to His will, and are supported by His gifts and blessings,* [it] is nevertheless not without sin.
Tappert: *Although we have God's Word and believe, although we obey and submit to his will and are supported by God's gift and blessing,* nevertheless we are not without sin.
Janzow: *Although we have the Word of God, believe in Him, obey Him, and submit to His will, and though His gifts and blessings nourish our lives,* yet we do not live without sinning.
K/W: *Although we have God's Word and believe, although we obey and submit to his will and are nourished by God's gift and blessing,* nevertheless we are not without sin.
Concordia: *Although we have and believe God's Word, do and submit to His will, and are supported by His gifts and blessings,* our life is still not sinless.

Henkel translates the clause with subjunctive mood verbs. He regarded the clause as hypothetical. The other translations are ambiguous about the mood of the verbs. Though the mood of the verbs is difficult to discern, ultimately the meaning is not greatly affected, since the concession is arguably true for the author.

CC33: Large Catechism IV 12 (subjunctive)

Henkel: But the Scripture teaches thus, that *even if all the works of the monks were collected in a mass*, no matter how precious they might appear, it would still not be as noble and good as if God lifts up a mite of straw.

Jacobs: But the Scriptures teach thus: *Even though we collect in one mass the works of all the monks*, however splendidly they may shine, they would not be as noble and good as if God should pick up a straw.

Lenker: But the Scriptures teach that *though we piled together all the works of all the monks*, however precious and dazzling they might appear, they would not have the value of a straw in comparison to God's works.

Triglotta: *Even though we collect in one mass the works of all the monks*, however splendidly they may shine, they would not be as noble and good as if God should pick up a straw.

Tappert: But the Scriptures teach that *if we piled together all the works of all the monks*, no matter how precious and dazzling they might appear, they would not be as noble and good as if God were to pick up a straw.

Janzow: But Scripture teaches that *even if we heaped together all the works of monks on one pile*, no matter how splendidly they might glitter, they would still not be as noble and good as the action of God if He were to pick up a piece of straw.

K/W: But the Scriptures teach that *if we piled together all the works of all the monks in a heap*, no matter how precious and dazzling they might appear, they would still not be as noble and good as if God were to pick up a straw.

Concordia: *Even if we collect in one pile the works of all the monks*, however splendidly they may shine, they would not be as noble and good as if God should pick up a single straw.

CC39: Large Catechism IV 54 (subjunctive)

Henkel: For *even if a Jew, at this day, should come with deceit and wicked design, and we should baptize him in all sincerity*, we should nevertheless say that the baptism would be right.

Jacobs: For *even though a Jew should to-day come with evil purpose and wickedness, and we should baptize him in all good faith*, we must say that his baptism is nevertheless genuine.

Lenker: *Even though a Jew came to us in our day with deceit and an evil purpose and we baptize him in all good faith*, we should have to admit that his baptism was genuine.

Triglotta: *Even though a Jew should to-day come dishonestly and with evil purpose, and we should baptize him in all good faith,* we must say that his baptism is nevertheless genuine.

Tappert: *Even though a Jew should today come deceitfully and with an evil purpose, and we baptized him in all good faith,* we should have to admit that his Baptism was valid.

Janzow: *For even though this very day a Jew were to come with deceitfulness and evil intent and we in good faith baptized him,* we would nevertheless have to affirm that the Baptism was valid.

K/W: *Even though a Jew should come today deceitfully and with an evil purpose, and we baptized him in good faith,* we ought to say that his baptism was nonetheless valid.

Concordia: *Suppose a Jewish person should come dishonestly and with evil intent, and we should baptize him in all good faith.*

CC42: Large Catechism IV 55 (subjunctive)

Henkel: For, as said, *even if children believe not,* which however is not the fact, (as now shown,) the baptism would still be right . . .

Jacobs: For (as we have said) *even though infants did not believe,* which, however, is not the case (as we shall now prove), yet their baptism would be genuine . . .

Lenker: As we said, *even if children do not believe*—which is proven not to be the case—yet their baptism would be valid . . .

Triglotta: For (as we have said) *even though infants did not believe,* which, however, is not the case, yet their baptism as now shown would be valid . . .

Tappert: As we said, *even if infants did not believe*—which, however, is not the case, as we have proved—still their Baptism would be valid . . .

Janzow: As we said, *even if infants did not believe* (which, however, is not the case, as we have proved), yet their Baptism would be valid . . .

K/W: As we said, *even if infants did not believe*—which, however, is not the case, as we have proved—still the baptism would be valid . . .

Concordia: As we have said, *even though infants did not believe* (which, however, is not the case), still their Baptism would be valid.

CC55: Smalcald Articles II IV 4 (indicative)

Henkel: All of which is nothing else but asserting, that *if even you believe in Christ, and are in possession of all things in him that are essential to salvation*, it avails nothing, and all is vain, if you do not hold me as your god, and are not subject and obedient to me.

Jacobs: All of which is nothing else than though it were said, that *although you believe in Christ, and have in him everything that is necessary to salvation*, yet nothing profits you . . .

Triglotta: *Although you believe in Christ, and have in Him [alone] everything that is necessary to salvation*, yet it is nothing and all in vain . . .

Tappert: *Although you believe in Christ, and in him have everything that is needful for salvation*, this is nothing and all in vain . . . .

K/W: *Even if you believe in Christ and have everything that is necessary for salvation in him*, nevertheless it is nothing . . . .

Concordia: *Although you believe in Christ and have in Him alone everything you need for salvation*, yet it is nothing and all in vain . . . .

This is a hypothetical situation, since Luther places the quote on the lips of the pope. In this case, by using the indicative, Luther heightens the rhetoric of the clause, making the pope state something that is patently ridiculous. The effect is satirical.

CC57: Smalcald Articles III VI 3 (subjunctive)

Henkel: For *even if it were true that there is as much in one element as in both*, still the one element is not the whole order and institution established and commanded by Christ.

Jacobs: For *although it may perhaps be true that there is as much under one as under both*, yet the one form is not the entire ordinance and institution established and commanded by Christ.

Triglotta: *Even if it were true that there is as much under one as under both*, yet the one form only is not the entire ordinance and institution [made] ordained and commanded by Christ.

Tappert: *Even if it were true that as much is included under one form as under both*, yet administration in one form is not the whole order and institution as it was established and commanded by Christ.

> **K/W**: *Even if it were true that there is as much under one kind as under both,* one kind is still not the complete order and institution as established and commanded by Christ.

> **Concordia**: *Even if that were true,* giving the one kind only is not the entire ordinance and institution commanded by Christ (Galatians 1:9).

Final tally for key examples (LC II 66 included)	
Indicative	4
Indicative or subjunctive	1
Subjunctive	9

OBSERVATIONS

The presence or lack of all-inclusive and exclusive terms proves highly important for determining the mood of the verb and the measure of the rhetoric. When such terms are present, the clauses have subjunctive verbs, with the exception of CC55. In this singular case, Luther creates a hypothetical statement and places it on the lips of the pope for absurd, satirical effect. The whole setting is contrary to fact. Luther chose the indicative mood here specifically for rhetorical affect.

Translators frequently chose the words "even if" when introducing the preceding clauses (33 times). The choice of "even if" has increased in the latest translations. This is likely because translators have grown more aware that "even if" better introduces concessive contrary-to-fact clauses for English readers. Also, please note a number of idiomatic ways translators have introduced these concessions:

- Let us grant . . .
- Even admitting . . .
- Even granting . . .
- Even if we were to concede . . .
- Even if it were the case . . .
- Suppose . . .

These idioms were used to amplify and illustrate the contrary to fact nature of the clauses they introduced.

NOTES

1. Many translations stem from the Jacobs translation (*Triglotta*, Tappert, K/W; *Concordia* is based on the *Triglotta*), so it is not surprising to see similarity in how the clauses were translated.
2. The ambiguity arises in part from changes in English usage and from strict literalness in translation. "English *though*, for instance, was still used in the sense of 'even if' at the time of Shakespeare, as the following quotation from Hamlet shows: *I'll speak to it though hell itself should gape and bid me hold my peace*. In Modern English, by contrast, *though* is used only in a factual, concessive sense, apart from certain relics like *as though*" (König, "Concessive Clauses," 822–23).
3. Lenker turns the concessive clause into a relative clause.
4. See Nordling, 239n17.

WORKS CITED

Anrich, Gustav. *Martin Bucer*. Strassburg: Karl J. Trübner, 1914.

Arand, Charles, and James Voelz. "Large Catechism, III, 66." *Concordia Journal* 29, no. 3 (July 2003): 232–34.

Baily, N., trans. *The Colloquies of Erasmus*. London: Reeves & Turner, 1878.

Die Bekenntnisschriften der evangelisch-lutherischen Kirche. 9th ed. Göttingen: Vanderhoeck & Ruprecht, 1967.

Bennett, J. "Even if." *Linguistics and Philosophy* 5 (1982).

Bente, F. *Historical Introductions to the Lutheran Confessions*. 2nd ed. St. Louis: CPH, 2005.

Bertram, Martin H. *Stimmen der Kirche*. St. Louis: CPH, 1961.

Bornkamm, Heinrich. *Luther's World of Thought*. St. Louis: CPH, 1958.

Brecht, Martin. *Martin Luther: His Road to Reformation*. Translated by James L. Schaaf. Vol. 1. Minneapolis: Fortress, 1985.

Brunner, Peter. *Worship in the Name of Jesus*. St. Louis: CPH, 1968.

Cassell's German-English, English-German Dictionary. New York: MacMillan Publishing Company, 1978.

Catechism of the Catholic Church. Mahwah, NJ: Paulist Press, 1994.

Chemnitz, Martin. *Loci Theologici*. St. Louis: CPH, 1989.

Corpus Reformatorum. Halis Saxonum: C.A. Schetschke, 1834–1860.

The Christian Book of Concord. Newmarket: Solomon D. Henkel and Brothers, 1851.

Concordia Theological Seminary. "Opinion of the Department of Systematic Theology: The Fruit of the Vine in the Sacrament of the Altar." *CTQ* 45, nos. 1–2 (January–April 1981).

Concordia: The Lutheran Confessions. St. Louis: CPH, 2005.

Dau, W. H. T., and F. Bente, eds. *Concordia Triglotta*. St. Louis: CPH, 1921.

Ebeling, Gerhard. *Wort und Glaube*. Vol. 2, Beiträge zur *Fundamentaltheologic und zur Lehre von Gott*. Tübingen, 1969.

Eells, Hastings. *Martin Bucer*. New Haven: Yale, 1931.

Elert, Werner. *The Structure of Lutheranism*. Translated by Walter A. Hansen. St. Louis: CPH, 1962.

———. *The Lord's Supper Today*. St. Louis: CPH, 1973.

———. *The Christian Faith: An Outline of Lutheran Dogmatics*. Columbus, OH: Lutheran Theological Seminary, 1974.

Encyclopedia Britannica, Macropaedia Vol. 15. 15th ed. Chicago: Encyclopedia Britannica, Inc., 1984.

Evangelische Bekenntnisse: Bekenntnisschriften der Reformation und neuere Theologische Erklarungen. Vol. 2. Bielefeld: Luther-Verlag, 1997.

The Faculty of Concordia Theological Seminary. "Religious Pluralism and Knowledge of the True God." *Concordia Theological Quarterly* 66, no. 4 (October 2002): 295–305.

Francisco, Adam S. *Martin Luther and Islam: A Study in Sixteenth Century Polemics and Apologetics*. Leiden: E. J. Brill, 2007.

Franke, Carl. *Grundzüge der Schriftsprache Luthers*. 3 vols. Halle: Der Buchhandlung des Waisenhauses, 1922.

Frye, Albert Myrton, and Albert William Levi. *Rational Belief: An Introduction to Logic*. New York: Harcourt, Brace and Company, 1941.

Grimm, Jacob, and Wilhelm Grimm. *Deutsches Wörterbuch*. Vol. 7. Leipzig: S. Hirzel, 1889.

Der Grosse Duden: Grammatik. Vol. 4. Mannheim/Zurich: Bibliographisches Institut, 1966.

Harless, G. C. A. *Commentar über den Brief Pauli an die Ephesier*. Erlangen: Carl Heyder, 1834.

Honderich, Ted, ed. *The Oxford Companion to Philosophy*. Oxford: Oxford University Press, 1995.

Hopper, Paul J., and Elizabeth Closs Traugott. *Grammaticalization*. Cambridge: Cambridge University Press, 1993.

Hutchinson, Jane Campbell. *Albrecht Dürer: A Biography*. Princeton: Princeton University Press, 1990.

Jacobs, Henry E., ed. *The Book of Concord*. Vol. 1. Philadelphia: Board of Publications of the General Council of the Evangelical Lutheran Church in North America, 1908.

Jannach, Hubert. *German for Reading Knowledge*. 3rd ed. Boston: Heinle & Heinle Publications, Inc., 1980.

Janzow, F. Samuel, trans. *Luther's Large Catechism*. St. Louis: CPH, 1978.

Kadai, Heino O. "Luther's Theology of the Cross." In *Accents in Luther's Theology*. St. Louis: CPH, 1967.

Kahn, Victoria. *Rhetoric, Prudence, and Skepticism in the Renaissance*. Ithaca, NY: Cornell University Press, 1985.

Kehrein, Joseph. *Grammatik der deutschen Sprache des funfzehnten bis siebenzehnten Jahrhunderts*. Vol. III. Hildsheim: Georg Olms, 1968.

Kneale, William and Martha. *The Development of Logic*. Oxford: Clarendon Press, 1975.

Knight, George T. *The New Schaff-Herzog Encyclopedia of Religious Knowledge*. Edited by S. M. Jackson. Vol. XII. Grand Rapids: Baker, 1950.

Kolb, Robert, and Timothy J. Wengert, eds. *The Book of Concord*. Minneapolis: Fortress, 2000.

König, Ekkehard. "Concessive Connectives and Concessive Sentences: Cross-Linguistic Regularities and Pragmatic Principles." In *Explaining Language Universals*, edited by John A. Hawkins. Oxford: Basil Blackwell Ltd., 1988.

————. "Concessive Clauses." In *Encyclopedia of Language and Literature*. 2nd ed. Vol. II. Oxford: Elsevier, 2006.

Kopff, E. Christian. "Who Believes in and Worships the One True God in Luther's Large Catechism?" *Logia: A Journal of Lutheran Theology* XIII, no. 3 (2004): 55–57.

Lanham, Richard A. *A Handlist of Rhetorical Terms*. 2nd ed. Berkeley: University of California Press, 1991.

Lenker, John Nicholas, trans. *Luther's Large Catechism*. Minneapolis: The Luther Press, 1908.

Locher, Gottfried W. *Zwingli's Thought: New Perspectives*. Leiden: E. J. Brill, 1981.

————. *Die Seligkeit erwählter Heiden bei Zwingli*. Zollikon, 1952.

. *Die Theologie Huldriych Zwinglis in Lichte seiner Christologie. Erster Teil: Die Gotteslehre*. Zürich: Zwingli-Verlag, 1952.

Lohnes, Walter F. W., and F. W. Strothmann. *German: A Structural Approach*. 3rd ed. New York: W. W. Norton & Company, 1980.

Lortz, Joseph. *The Reformation in Germany*. 2 vols. New York: Herder and Herder, 1968.

Luther, Martin. *The Table Talk of Martin Luther*. Edited by Thomas S. Kepler. Grand Rapids: Baker, 1952.

Luthers Werke. Weimar: Hermann Böhlau, 1912.

Manteufel, Thomas. "What Luther Meant." *Concordia Journal*, October 2003.

Matheson, Peter. *The Rhetoric of the Reformation*. Edinburgh: T & T Clark LTD, 1998.

Mau, R. *Evangelische Bekenntnisse: Bekenntnisschriften der Reformation und neuere Theologische Erklärungen*. Vol. 2. Bielefeld: Luther-Verlag, 1997.

Meola, Claudio Di. *Der Audsdruck der Konzessivatät in der deutschen Gegenwartssprache: Theorie und Beschreibung anhand eines Vergleichs mit dem Italienischen*. Tübingen: Max Niemeyer Verlag, 1997.

————. "Synchronic Variation as a Result of Grammaticalization: Concessive Subjunctives in German and Italian." *Linguistics* 39–1 (2001).

More, Thomas. *Utopia: A New Translation, Backgrounds, Criticism*. Translated by Robert M. Adams. New York: W. W. Norton & Company.

Muret-Sanders Encyclopädisches Wörterbuch der englischen und deutschen Sprache. Vol. II. Berlin: Langenscheidtsche Verlagsbuchhandlung, 1905.

Murphy, James J. *Rhetoric in the Middle Ages*. Berkeley: University of California Press, 1974.

Murray, Peter and Linda. *The Oxford Companion to Christian Art and Architecture*. Oxford: Oxford University Press, 1996.

Nordling, John. "Large Catechism III, 66, Latin Version" *Concordia Journal* (July 2003).

Oberman, Heiko A. *The Harvest of Medieval Theology: Gabriel Biel and Late Medieval Nominalism*. Durham, NC: The Labyrinth Press, 1983.

The Oxford Dictionary of the Christian Church. 2nd ed. Oxford: Oxford University Press, 1983.

The Oxford-Duden German Dictionary. Rev. ed. Oxford: Clarendon Press, 1997.

Pieper, Francis. *Christian Dogmatics*. Vol. III. St. Louis: CPH, 1953.

Pöhlmann, Horst Georg, ed. *Unser Glaube: Die Bekenntnisschriften der evangelisch-lutherische Kirche*. 3rd ed. Gütersloher: Gütersloher Verlagshaus Gerd Mohn, 1991.

Potter, G. R. *Zwingli*. Cambridge: Cambridge University Press, 1976.

WORKS CITED

Ramsey, Violeta. "The Functional Distribution of Preposed and Postponed 'If' and 'When' Clauses in Written Discourse." In *Coherence and Grounding in Discourse*, edited by Russell S. Tomlin. Philadelphia: John Benjamins Publishing Company, 1987.

Reu, M. *Luther's German Bible*. Columbus, OH: The Lutheran Book Concern, 1934.

Ross, James F., and Bates, Todd. "Duns Scotus on Natural Theology." In *The Cambridge Companion to Duns Scotus*, edited by Thomas Williams. Cambridge: Cambridge University Press, 2003.

Sanders, Daniel. *Wörterbuch der Hauptschwierigkeiten in der deutschen Sprache*. Berlin: Langenscheidtsche Verlags-Buchhandlung, 1894.

Sasse, Hermann. *This Is My Body*. Adelaide: Lutheran Publishing House, 1959.

Schaff, Philip. *History of the Christian Church*. 8 vols. Grand Rapids: Eerdmans, 1984 reprint.

———. *The Creeds of Christendom*. 6th ed. 3 vols. Grand Rapids: Baker, 1990 reprint.

Smith, Glenn D. "A Rhetorical Biography: An Analysis of Selected Sermons Preached by Martin Luther." PhD diss., University of Nebraska, August 1971.

Spitz, Lewis W. *The Renaissance and Reformation Movements, Revised Edition*. St. Louis: CPH, 1987.

Stephens, W. P. *The Theology of Huldrych Zwingli*. Oxford: Clarendon Press, 1986.

Stolt, Birgit. *Martin Luthers Rhetorik des Herzens*. Tübingen: Mohr Siebeck, 2000.

Sturtz, Henry. *501 German Verbs*. New York: Barron's, 1982.

Tappert, Theodore G., ed. *The Book of Concord*. Philadelphia: Fortress, 1959.

Tyoeinoja, Reijo. "Proprietas Verbi: Luther's Conception of Philosophical and Theological Language in the Disputation: Verbum caro factum est (Joh. 1:14), 1539." In *Faith, Will, and Grammar: Some Themes of Intensional Logic and Semantics in Medieval and Reformation Thought*, edited by Heikki Kirjavainen. Helsinki: Luther-Agricola-Society, 1986.

Wörterbuch der deutschen Gegenwartssprache. Vol. 4. Berlin: Akademie-Verlag, 1974.

Zwingli, Ulrich. *On Providence and Other Essays*. Durham, NC: The Labyrinth Press, 1983.